Also by Ronald Hirsch

The Self in No Self: Buddhist Heresies and Other Lessons of a Buddhist Life

We STILL Hold These Truths: Preserving the Heart of American Democracy for the 21st Century

Making Your Way In Life As a Buddhist

A Practical Guide

Ronald Hanh Niêm Hirsch

ThePracticalBuddhist.com Publishing

Published 2012 by ThePracticalBuddhist.com Publishing, Stuyvesant, NY 12173. U.S. © 2011-2012 Ronald L. Hirsch. All rights reserved.

No part of this publication may be reproduced, stored in a retrieval system, or transmitted in any form or by any means, electronic, mechanical, recording or otherwise, without the prior written permission of Ronald L. Hirsch

ISBN   978-0-98832-902-7   (softcover),   978-0-98832-903-4 (eBook)

To my best friend and companion, Ken,
who with unfailing love and compassion
supports me in all that I do,
encourages me to make the most of myself,
and provides me with valuable counsel
to help me along the path.

TABLE OF CONTENTS

Preface: We Are Not Enlightened, Ergo …		1
1	Building a Platform of Serenity	5
	I Believe – The Importance of Faith	7
	Aware Breath = Instant Samadhi	10
	The Power of Smiling Mindfully	13
	Take Joy in Each Moment, in Everything You Do	16
	Accepting Ourselves –	
	Cultivating a Compassionate Heart	19
	Accepting Life	27
	Staying Grounded	34
2	How Does a Buddhist Think About the Future?	41
	How To Plan Yet Remain Present?	42
	How to Desire Yet Not Crave?	44
3	Personal Life	49
	How to Love	49
	Sex	58
	Family Relationships	66
	Others	75
	Death	79
	When You're Feeling Down	82
	When Really Bad Things Happen	84
4	"Work"	87
	Choosing Your Purpose in Life	87
	Moving Your Career Forward	97
	Workplace Relationships	99
5	Lifestyle	101
	Meat or No Meat	102
	Drinking, Reading, Watching, Listening	105
	You As Consumer	109
	Your Environmental Impact	111
	Charity/Volunteer Work	116
6	Your Buddhist Practice	119

Preface:
We Are Not Enlightened, Ergo

If we were all enlightened or boddhisatvas, there would be no need for this book. Dwelling in perfected wisdom, free of ego, at one with all things, experiencing things, observing, without the intervention of thought we would have returned to our self-natures ... our true Buddha nature. Our minds would be one with the way. And when our minds are one with the way, nothing in the world offends, obstructions cease to be, thought objects disappear for things are things because of mind as mind is mind because of things; both at source are empty of intrinsic existence. Without opinions pro and con, without the mind's discrimination, we clearly see the truth.[1] There is only one way forward.

But most of us are not enlightened nor do we have the realistic prospect of becoming enlightened in the near or perhaps even distant future. Even reaching a stage approaching enlightenment is very difficult. Yet each day, we are faced with countless moments when we need to make decisions about how we lead our lives ... whether they concern our work, our personal relationships, or our lives in general. What voice will we listen to ... our ego or our true Buddha nature?

We cannot escape the fact that we are part of the contemporary culture. Enlightened or not, we live in this world and it is the way it is. We are part of it ... our work, our shopping, our reading, our family relationships ... all of this happens within the context of and is impacted by our

---

[1] Roshi Philip Kapleau, *Chants,* "Affirming Faith in Mind," Rochester Zen Center, 1990

culture. And it is this context that forms our ego, which is the sum of all our learned experience. But we cannot conform our lives to the teachings of this culture if we are walking the Buddhist path and hope to experience wellbeing, in the sense of peace and contentment.[2]

The question then is, if we wish to live our lives as a Buddhist, how do we make our decisions in a way that is consistent with our practice? How do we stay on the path, rather than constantly fall off of it because of the pull of our ego.

This is of critical importance to a Buddhist because Buddhism is a way of life. If you meditate everyday and go to temple, but otherwise live your life as others do in our culture, then you are not really a practicing Buddhist. (As an aside, I would say the same for those who profess to be Christians, Jews, or adherents of any of the world's major religions.)

The simple answer is to be mindful, aware, and always make decisions from a place of equanimity with reference to the five Precepts.[3] But while the answer is simple, I know from my own messy experience that the practical application of it is far from simple.

---

[2] This view is not accepted by some others who feel that the inherent dissonances between Buddhism and Western culture can be resolved through an accommodation between the two. For example, in his otherwise excellent and helpful book, *Buddhist Practice on Western Ground*, Harvey Aronson does not accept that one must abandon various Western cultural markings in order to fully practice the Buddha dharma. He argues that one can have the best of both worlds. I would say as regards the issues he addresses … self, love, anger, and attachment … that the only answer is to free ourselves from our Western way of thinking and follow the Buddha dharma, properly viewed.

[3] The Five Precepts are rules or trainings, not imperatives like the Ten Commandments, that lay people vow to practice when they formally commit themselves to Buddhism. At their core they are about not harming others or oneself and helping when one can. The ceremony is called, "taking the Precepts."

First, we find it very hard to be mindful throughout the day. It's hard enough while we're meditating! All too often I would find myself mindful after the fact, after I had acted in a decidedly unmindful manner. That may make for a teachable moment, but the damage has already been done. How do we increase our mindfulness throughout the day?

Second, for the most part we are not in a space of equanimity. Our ego pulls us in a variety of directions; we are filled with cravings and attachments and dissatisfaction with the way things are right now. And so I typically made my decisions in an irrational way, even if the form of rationality was adhered to. How then, I thought, can I increase my equanimity while still in the grasp of my ego?

The first chapter of the book, "Building a Platform of Serenity," addresses these issues. It provides a practical path to increase ones mindfulness and equanimity while still being in an unenlightened state.

If you think that is difficult, the real challenge is living life as a Buddhist. Chapters 2 through 5 offer practical examples of the types of situations we face in our daily lives that require decisions and suggest how they can be traversed in a manner that is consistent with our Buddhist path.

This is no simple matter for we will often ... no, almost always ... be pulled in the opposite direction by the habit energy of our culture, by our ego, and by friends and family. I cannot overstate the radical shift that is involved for most of us when we choose to apply Buddhist principles to all aspects of our lives.

Much of what I have to say may strike you as bizarre or unrealistic, but that is only because we are so used to thinking about these issues in a way that is informed by our culture and the environment we grew up in. If you truly seek to live your life as a Buddhist, you will take what I say to heart, uncomfortable or inconvenient though the implications may often be.

The book ends with a chapter on Buddhist practice ... the formal part, that is. For as noted above, as a Buddhist, your whole life, every day, every moment, is an integral part of your practice.

Following the path is not an easy process. We are trying to change the paradigms of our life, and that requires great discipline and patience.

And while meditation is central to the process, it cannot bring an end to our suffering on its own. It is the context of the Buddha dharma that makes meditation powerful. I remember once reading that a practitioner said to a monk, "I've been meditating for 20 years and nothing has changed!" Perhaps that was because she had been meditating but not absorbing the teachings of the Buddha.

And even then, the clarity that one hopefully achieves while meditating does not magically apply itself to your daily life or end your suffering. It is only through purposeful actions and a disciplined practice (meaning how you approach your whole life) that you can make practical application of the clarity you receive while meditating to daily events.

There is light at the end of the tunnel if you follow the path and incorporate the teachings *as best you can* in your daily activities and your life choices.

Chapter 1
Building a Platform Of Serenity

Serenity. What a completely foreign concept this was to me. How can anyone be serene unless they're a saint? All I'd known in my life was constant inner turmoil, certainly since I was a young child. And in looking around at my peers and family, and at the images of the larger culture, I didn't see anyone who was serene. My parents may have been in love, and friends laughed and relaxed, but that's not serenity. Everyone was beset with problems that disturbed them. Even in the idealistic sitcoms of the 50s, whether it was the Beaver, or Ozzie and Harriet, or Lucy ... everyone's lives were filled with conflict and confusion. Yet I knew in my gut that serenity and a life free of suffering was a rational, reasonable goal. The question was not whether, but how?

. . . .

I had been a practicing Buddhist for several years, but my practice was not progressing. My life was definitely calmer, but my mind was not quiet, even when sitting on my cushion. I had been going to temple, but the teaching was not challenging and didn't move me forward on the path.

What I had learned about the basics of Buddhist philosophy through reading, however, motivated me to go deeper with my practice. It all made sense to me, and yet it was so foreign to my experience and our culture that I knew making progress would not be easy.

Just as space explorers need to go to an orbiting platform before venturing into deep space, I felt I needed to create a platform of serenity upon which to build further explorations of my mind. That serenity is also essential to maintaining the calm abiding in which to make daily life decisions that are consistent with the path.

I had thought that serenity would come as a natural product of meditation. But although I meditated daily, it didn't seem to increase my serenity.

For meditation to "work", I realized that not only is it important to create a physical atmosphere that is calm, it is important to have a psyche that, if not abidingly calm, at least is not in constant turmoil. Otherwise, try as I may to focus on my breathing during meditation, my mind would be bombarded with thoughts of the unfinished business of my life; my ego would not give me much rest. I was perhaps calm during meditation, but I did not experience much peace.

And so I slowly built a platform of serenity based on the steps outlined in the following sections. It is a practical, realizable approach. It speaks to the goal of attaining a serenity that enables one to begin experiencing peace, happiness, and hope in the present by beginning to lift obstructions and frustration from your mind and soul ... a serenity we need to make skillful decisions in our lives and the peace necessary for the deeper exploration of our mind.[4]

---

[4] This material appears in essentially the same form in my other books, *The Self in No Self: Buddhist Heresies and Other Lessons of a Buddhist Life* and *Scratching the Itch: Getting to the Root of Our Suffering*. It is included in each because building a platform of serenity is an essential step in making progress on the path.

I BELIEVE – THE IMPORTANCE OF FAITH

Because following the Buddhist path means going against the grain of almost everything in our learned experience, everything our ego and our culture tells us, I quickly found that it is not a walk in the park. It requires commitment, discipline and patience. And to be able to apply those three practices in the face of the obstacles and struggles we face daily requires deep faith ... faith in the teachings of the Buddha.

For many people, "faith" is a loaded word from their religious upbringing. But faith, or belief, in the Buddha dharma is qualitatively different from the faith that is sought in most religious contexts. Religious faith often requires belief in something that flies in the face of reason. Whether it's a belief in God, or belief in the virgin birth and resurrection of Jesus, or the Trinity, or the countless miracles ... all of these things require what's often called a "leap of faith" or sometimes "blind faith."

In Buddhism, the situation is different. In Buddhism there is no God; there is no creation story ... things just are. When most of us read a Buddhist text or listen to a good dharma talk, we respond by saying, "Of course, that makes such perfect sense. I can relate that so well to what I've experienced." In general, our intellect is on board rather quickly with our following the Buddhist path.

For Buddhists, it is the ego, our habit energy, that must be successfully countered if we are to make progress on the path. When the core of my ego screamed at me, "I want!" as I worked to be grateful for the wonderful things in my life or accept my life as it is now, it was only my deep faith in the teachings of the Buddha that provided me with the strength to say to my ego, "no."

That faith has two main components. The first is faith that the path provided by the Buddha dharma will end our suffering ... provided that we have the strength to follow it.

That sounds like it should be simple. That is, after all, why we are Buddhists. Yes, there are many other features of Buddhism that make it attractive to us, but it is the desire to end our suffering that keeps us persevering.

And yet having deep faith in our chosen path is not simple. That is because at this stage of our practice we are still primarily creatures of the ego, of feelings, of perceptions; our true Buddha nature, our unborn mind is virtually a stranger to us. And the sum of our learned experience in the form of our ego will throw every thing it can at us to subvert us from the path. Only by staying focused on my faith in the teachings was I able to withstand this sometimes seemingly relentless pressure.

The other main component is faith in our own true Buddha nature. While this concept doesn't fly in the face of reason, it doesn't easily respond to the intellect either.

There are many rationale that compromise our belief in our true Buddha nature. One is, if we were born with our true Buddha nature and it's still there, why has it allowed us to suffer so? Why doesn't it show itself more clearly, even when we are searching for it? We often find this hard to grasp.

For those brought up in the Christian faith, another problem is the concept of original sin ... the exact opposite of the Buddhist belief. If you had the concept of being born a sinner drummed into your head in church during your formative years, it's understandable that the concept of being born perfect would be a challenging, albeit a welcomed, one.

Finally, because for most of us our true Buddha nature has been buried under the many layers of learned experience that form our ego, the fact that it is not visible to us, that we can't touch it somehow, is an obstacle to our belief. We have to take it as a matter of faith, until we are sufficiently aware that we begin to see glimpses of our true Buddha nature revealed to us. This happens when we begin observing without the intervention of thought[5] and we become aware of the discrepancy between what our ego is whispering in our ear about something and what our true Buddha nature is telling us.

Sometimes, visualization can be an important aid in understanding or projecting something. I had been trying for some time while meditating to somehow connect with my true Buddha nature, to visualize this non-physical thing, to no avail. Then one day, as I was meditating, I suddenly saw before me smiling, laughing images of me as a toddler. I knew immediately that there was my true Buddha nature, taking joy in the moment for no particular reason, full of love, an innocent in the world unburdened by learned experience. Not uncoincidently I'm sure, I had within the previous few months received from my mother both my baby book and an album of photos of me as a baby and toddler!

But at bottom, if we believe in the teachings of the Buddha, then we believe that each of us is born with our true Buddha nature intact and that it remains a part of us forever ... the one thing that is not impermanent and changeable.

Armed by our faith, there will be a counterforce within us whenever our ego tries to get us to give up the path or question it.

---

[5] As will be discussed later on, it is not that one doesn't have thoughts, but that one doesn't attach to them or engage them, and therefore they do not intervene in our observations.

AWARE BREATH = INSTANT SAMADHI

It's all fine and well being in a calm, peaceful state when one is meditating, sitting on ones cushion, but what happens while we're going through the rest of the day? Remaining in that state while encountering all the stressors of everyday life seemed an impossible challenge to me. Meditation became a time-bound refuge, not an every-moment lifestyle.

The usual advice regarding this problem is to be mindful throughout the day, to observe, to be aware. Unfortunately for most of us, mindfulness always seems to come after the event, after we have reacted to something in a decidedly unmindful way. While this makes for a teachable moment, it does not help us much in the process of establishing a mindful state throughout the day.

The problem is one of focus. When we sit on our cushion to meditate, we learn from the outset to focus on our breathing ... breathing in, breathing out ... not to cut out what is happening around us or the thoughts that flow through our minds, but just to be aware of those things while focusing on our breath. This allows us to be mindful. But when we are not sitting, meditating, our minds are focused on all the various things happening around us.

One day while I was sitting, I practiced breathing in a way suggested by an article I had recently read ... I felt my breath come in as I expanded my diaphragm, rise up through my lungs, expand my upper back muscles, and then descend again to my diaphragm when I exhaled. As I practiced this method of breathing, and observed it, the image came to me that my breath was like a wave washing gently over my body. And just as waves cleanse the sand, so too my breath ... the breath of life ... was cleansing my body and soul.

I understood then that focusing on our breathing while meditating is not just a tool to help us stay focused; the awareness of breathing in and out is the basic building block of meditation. I realized that with each *aware* breath, regardless whether we are sitting on our cushion meditating or out and about, we are mindful, evils are extinguished, karma is purified, and obstructions dissolved.

But the question then became, how to achieve that awareness when I'm not sitting. When we sit to meditate, we are doing something purposeful that makes it easy ... well, easier ... to focus on our breathing. What we need to do, at least in the beginning, is to do something similarly purposeful to focus us at various points throughout the day.

The first step is to purposefully stop whatever you're doing, mentally and physically, for a moment or a few. Because if you don't stop you can't take the next step and focus on your spirituality.

In Korean Zen, there are various chants/exercises based on the word, ma-um, which means, "mind." One of the exercises is, "breathing in we say 'ma,' which relaxes the body, breathing out we say 'um,' which relaxes the mind." This was something I could do periodically throughout the day, I thought.

And what I've found is that after doing the exercise (3 times in succession), I not only am aware of my breath, but I am instantly in the relaxed peaceful state that I experience when sitting on my cushion meditating. I may remain in that state, focused on my breathing, for as few as a few breaths or as long as several minutes, depending on what's going on around me.

Another technique that has worked for me is just saying the mantra, "Breathing in, I am aware that I am breathing in. Breathing out, I am aware that I am breathing out." Again, saying this 3 times in succession has brought me to a quiet, meditative state.

Once you are in a meditative state, and thus centered, observe whether you are or, more importantly, have been just prior to your entering this meditative state, in a state of equanimity, whether you feel compassion for yourself and others, whether you have been observing ... that is *not* engaging ... your feelings, whether you are accepting of yourself and the world around you.

If the answer to any of these queries is, "no," then if the situation allows, continue to meditate to regain the state of equanimity. If the situation does not allow continued meditation, at least you will be aware that you are not in a state of equanimity and be mindful of your actions and thoughts.

It may not sound like much, but these on-the-feet mini-meditations have enabled me to be more mindful throughout the day. Try it ... you'll like it.

THE POWER OF SMILING MINDFULLY

Most of us are frustrated or at least concerned about many aspects of our lives, both large and small. So when we hear or read that the teaching of Buddhism says to accept things as being the way they are because it's just the way it is, we have a problem with that teaching. I certainly pushed back against it initially because I did not *want* to accept things as being the way they are ... even for a moment. I may have said, "I accept," but I didn't really accept.

On the one hand, I had approached Buddhism because I wanted to end my suffering, but on the other hand I really didn't want to do what I had to do to end that suffering. I feared the unknown ... if I accepted things as they are, then how would I pursue the rest of my life?[6]

While nothing can take the place of meditation in removing these obstructions and bringing us closer to acceptance, there is a shortcut to at least lessen the frustration and thereby ease that barrier ... smiling mindfully.

As you go through the day, try to be aware of your facial expression. If you're like me, you'll find that in general your facial muscles are either frowning or in a serious repose. This is our usual state when we're alone with our thoughts as opposed to being engaged in conversation with others or being entertained.

I regret that it was only after years of Buddhist practice and experiencing in general a state of peace and contentment that I became aware one day that most of the time my facial muscles were tense. And as I observed my tense facial muscles, I became aware that this tenseness created a state of non-joy that was at odds with the peace and contentment that I was otherwise experiencing.

---

[6] For more on this, see the section, "The Desire That Is Right Desire," in my book, *The Self in No Self: Buddhist Heresies and Other Lessons of a Buddhist Life.*

Purposefully, I brought a smile to my face and found that this in turn brought an immediate uplift to my spirits. Just releasing the facial tension made me feel lighter and filled with happiness. This is what Thich Nhat Hanh calls "mouth yoga." But I found that the smile and its impact were fleeting because it was mechanical and I was quickly distracted.

Then one day while meditating, I realized that if I were able to be aware every moment of the wonderful things in my life right then at each moment, without attaching, I would smile mindfully and naturally every moment. Even if I was focused on some concern of mine, I would at the same time be mindful of the things that brought joy to my life.

Well, every moment was perhaps too much to expect at the start. But every moment I was aware of my breath, I would say to myself, "I am grateful for all the wonderful things in my life right now at this moment," and as those things came to mind I could feel myself smiling. As time passed, I observed that my awareness of the good things in my life began to permeate my day and I smiled more, not just when I was aware of my breath.

But this experience raised a question in my mind ... if I was generally in a state of peace and contentment, then why was the default status of my face a frown or serious expression?

Generally we frown for various reasons ... our culture is so focused on wanting what we don't have (not necessarily something material) and on proving ourselves through competition, we are so attached to the past and obsessed with the future, and the problems of the world around us are so vexing, that most of us are in an almost constant state of some degree of frustration or concern, whether consciously or not. If we are frustrated, we are not happy, and that agitation shows in our facial expression.

Was my frowning a sign of the deep underlying frustration and insecurity in my gut that my practice had not yet touched? Were the troubles of the world and especially U.S. politics so overburdening? As a Buddhist I derive joy from the happiness of others, but the corollary is also true, I derive sadness from the pain of others.

Or was this default position merely a product of decades of negative muscle training brought about by my samsara-filled life?[7] I know from my baby photos and family anecdotes that before I was burdened by my ego and learned experience I always had a smile on my face. My father called me his "sunshine."

My hunch was "all of the above." Of course this practice of smiling mindfully did not change my underlying condition or the reality of the world with its problems. But it did provide me with a renewed focus on the positive in my life and increased my experience of joy and happiness.

The strengthening of this positive perspective brought me back to basics, opening me up to more fully accepting things as being the way they are, releasing obstructions, and going deep within myself in meditation. By doing so, it gave me more energy to tackle the challenges of life with Right view, free of illusion.

---

[7] Samsara is the endless cycle of suffering caused by our ego-driven unskillful actions and emotions/reactions.

TAKE JOY IN EACH MOMENT, IN EVERYTHING YOU DO

A monk once said to me, "Take joy, Ron, in each moment, in everything you do."

In our culture, we are programmed to seek out things to do that will be fun. Whether it's going out and buying something, going to some cultural event, taking a trip, or countless other options. The point is, to do something other than what we are currently doing, something that is not required of us or part of our daily routine.

We always want something different, something new, to stimulate us. The result is that we take little or no joy in the everyday aspects of our lives. How sad when right before our eyes, every moment of every day, there is something to take joy in and value. It's all a matter of perspective.

For years I paid no attention to the monk's simple teaching and my life was very unsettled despite a disciplined practice of daily meditation and reading. Then one day while I was meditating, this teaching came to mind and I let it sit there while I observed it and took its measure. It was one of those "eureka" moments. I resolved from that day onward, at first purposefully, to do as the monk had taught.

To take joy in each moment, one must first be present in the moment. If your thinking about this and that ... what you're going to be doing later in the day, how some problem will resolve itself, whatever ... then you can't take joy in the moment because that requires the focus of being present. There's a time for those thoughts, but it's not when you're getting dressed or doing laundry; it's when you sit down purposefully to think about those things because you need to be present for those thoughts as well.

I remember that first day well. Purposefully, I was present in each moment, something that was surprisingly rare for me despite my years of practice and disciplined daily meditation; such is the power of our mind. Everything I did, from the most mundane tasks of washing and drying the dishes or feeling the soft material of a knit top as I pulled it on to more mentally challenging tasks such as reading to just looking out and seeing the wind play with the grasses, tossing their seed heads this way and that in an undulating ballet ... I literally took joy in every moment, in everything I did.

This practice is enhanced when you are able to experience, to observe what you do and the world around you directly, without the intervention of thought. When the negative labels are gone, you will, for example, be able to see the gray, rainy day for the wonderful, complex, interesting day that it is rather than a "gloomy" or "ugly" day. Even before you get to that point in your practice, however, just being aware of the labels and choosing to see what else is there makes a big difference.

Whether you live in the country or the city, are rich or poor, are educated or not, this practice is available to all. When you are doing a task, even a very repetitive or menial one, or just being you have a choice whether to be bored or take joy.

Be aware of the motions of your body or the actions of your mind in accomplishing that task and strive to do the best you can in accomplishing it. Do it purposefully, not carelessly; give it thought, give it structure, give it dignity. Be aware of the layers of texture and the countless minute miracles of nature or science that are involved in your being able to accomplish the task well or just in your being alive. No task is mindless; no moment is without wonder and dignity.

When you are out and about, whether walking down a crowded city street or walking through a country meadow, let all your senses be alive with the experience, free of thought. Let's say you're walking in the city. You have a choice whether to focus on the dirt and noise and traffic and find it depressing, or feel the energy, the diversity of people, the amazing fact that somehow all of this works in unison. Likewise if you're walking in the country on a very hot summer day, you have the choice to focus on how uncomfortable you feel because of the heat or you can focus on the hugely varied texture and miracle of nature that is available to your senses.

In a way, this practice can be thought of as a further step in the practice of smiling mindfully. When we begin that practice and think of the wonderful things in our life, we typically think of larger, more significant things that play a major role in our lives. In this practice, we realize that all the minutiae of our lives are full of wonder and available to take joy in; we are aware of the dignity of our lives. And being present provides the access, the door to experiencing that joy and dignity.

ACCEPTING OURSELVES – CULTIVATING A COMPASSIONATE HEART

For years I wandered through my life frustrated. It didn't matter whether I was doing something I enjoyed or whether I was keeping up with what was happening in the world. What I enjoyed awakened cravings that left me anxious and frustrated. What disturbed me in the world left me feeling angry and agitated. And of course not having what I wanted left me frustrated. The problem was that I was approaching everything in my life from a place that lacked equanimity.

If we want to be in this world and not be agitated by all the terrible things that are happening, if we want to do the things we enjoy and give our life purpose without awakening cravings and frustration, if we want to feel at peace and content, there is one clear answer ... acceptance.[8] Until I truly accepted myself and my life as it was right then and accepted the world as it was right then, I was constantly subject to the suffering, the agony, caused by craving, frustration, and anger.

The first step is to accept *ourselves* ... to have compassion for ourselves and love ourselves unconditionally. For myself, as for so many people, learning to love myself unconditionally and have compassion for myself was a real challenge.

Why is it so hard for us to have compassion for ourselves? One would think that compassion would be a significant coping mechanism. But our ego, while supportive of every manner of rationalization to justify our actions or our failure to act, does not allow us to feel

---

[8] That is, this is the answer if one is not at the stage of practice where one has understood the illusory nature of all perceptions and the impermanence of all things, is free of your ego, and realized nonattachment. At that point acceptance is not an issue because there is nothing to accept; you and the world around you are one, free of labels, everything just is.

compassion and unconditional love for ourselves because that would undermine the power of the learned labels that it ruthlessly applies to us.

"Wait," you say, "I have felt pity towards myself or sorrow at my condition." But pity and sorrow are not compassion, at least not in the Buddhist sense. Because pity and sorrow do not negate the underlying condition as perceived by our ego. It does not change the perception that we are bad or a failure or whatever.

"Well, what about all the people out there with huge egos? Are you saying they don't love themselves?" They may love themselves, but certainly not unconditionally and they don't have compassion for themselves. People with huge egos have been shown to be at bottom very insecure people. The huge ego is a façade that hides their insecurity.

For a Buddhist, the origin of compassion is love, whether for oneself or others. It is selfless and unconditional. When compassion flows from unconditional love, we do not judge ourselves anymore. We accept ourselves for what we are ... without labels.

So how do we cultivate unconditional love and compassion while still in the throes of our ego? The answer comes in two parts ... one organic, one intellectual.

Before we understand the illusory nature of all perceptions, before we have freed ourselves from the past and the future, before we are free of our ego, we come to believe in our own true Buddha nature ... that faith that I discussed in the first section of this chapter ... and we understand samsara.

We come to know early on in our practice that our samsara ... the particular combination of cravings and neuroses that we suffer from ... is the result of our learned experience. We become aware that our self-image is actually a reflection of the image others have had of us, not a reflection of unfiltered reality ... for example, we may not make much money or have much, but we are not a "failure;" we may be gay, but we're not "weird" or "sick;" we may be overweight, but we are not "fat;" we may have plain looks, but we're not "homely;" those are labels set by our culture, our peers, or our family. Even fear, guilt, and shame are learned as children. All our thoughts are molded by our learned experience.

And we come to an awareness of our, in a very basic sense, limited control over our lives when we may have thought we were quite in control of things. We are products of our environment and upbringing, and the way we are programmed by those factors limits in a very practical way the choices our mind can make.

At this stage of our practice, however, despite our intellectual awareness of these truths, we are not free of these feelings; we are not free of our ego. Our true Buddha nature is unknown to us.

But that awareness does allow us to challenge the thoughts we've had about ourselves through the organic process of affirmations. Affirmations are designed to displace our negative learned feelings and labels with positive ones that reflect our inner being, our true Buddha nature. Obviously the very fact that one needs to recite affirmations, at least in the beginning, indicates that part of you doesn't really believe them. In order not to get caught in that trap ... that is, affirming what you don't believe and thus perversely reinforcing that disbelief ... it is of critical importance that part of you *does* believe what you are affirming, whether it's your unconditional love for yourself or your true Buddha nature and that you acknowledge at least intellectually that all the thoughts you have about yourself are labels that reflect the judgment of family or culture, they do not reflect the real you. It is important that part of you can honestly say, "yes," to each of your affirmations and that you vocalize them with conviction.

In essence, what you are doing with affirmations is having an intervention with your ego. You are telling your ego, just as the Buddha might tell Mara, his spirit tempter, that you are going to pursue the path of peace and contentment and that you will not be deflected from this path with negative feelings. While doing this, always have compassion for your ego for it is part of you. The point is to empower yourself to follow the path you have chosen and that your heart knows is right by freeing yourself from your negative thoughts.[9]

Recognizing the power of my ego and the entrenched nature of these negative feelings, I began many years ago reciting affirmations. At first, I recited them while giving myself a bear-hug, which I found very powerful and cathartic. Later I began reciting affirmations together with other mantras each morning while doing my walking meditation prior to sitting.

Here are some examples of affirmations that either I have used or have given to others to use:

I, Ron, love, respect, and accept myself unconditionally.
YES, I love myself no matter what I do or have done, what I say or have said, what I possess, who I am with, whether I am alone, whether I am acknowledged or not, whether I work – no matter what, I love and respect myself unconditionally

---

[9] If for whatever reason you cannot yet even acknowledge these truths, then you are indeed in a rough spot. You have chosen to follow the Buddhist path to end your suffering, but you cannot end that suffering while holding on to your negative feelings. Every step forward will sooner rather than later be met with a step backward; you will have a few days of peace and then the ugly head of anger will rise up and assert itself. I know it's not that you *want* to hold on to these negative feelings, but their habit-energy has you captive.

If, like most of us, you are here, trying to follow the Buddhist path, because you responded positively to teaching that you read or heard, you need to reconnect with whatever moved you and meditate on finding faith in the teachings of the Buddha, which as stated earlier is critical to making progress on the path. Meditate on acknowledging the truths of samsara.

> and have compassion for myself. I believe in my true Buddha nature.

> I, Ron, am a good person.

> I, Ron, am loved, valued, and needed by others. My existence makes a difference in this world.

> My feelings of inadequacy or failure reflect cultural or family judgments. They have no intrinsic existence; they are mere labels that are a product of my mind.

> My inner being is always at peace and happy even when something happens to disturb me, just like the sun is always shining and the sky is always blue even when it is cloudy.

I continue to recite affirmations and mantras to this day because ones practice needs to be disciplined. Even though my affirmations now do reflect my unequivocal, honest awareness about myself, one must be ever vigilant and aware that negative feelings may still occasionally arise even after years of practice, especially in a moment of weakness.

Another organic approach to cultivating unconditional love and compassion for oneself is to follow the instructions of Sogyal Rinpoche and first "unseal the spring of loving kindness" towards yourself and then practice "tonglen" on yourself ... the Tibetan practice of taking on the suffering and pain of others and giving them your happiness, well-being, and peace of mind.[10]

Sogyal Rinpoche recommends starting this practice by first doing it for yourself. Before one can have such compassion for others, one has to have compassion for oneself. The first step is to *"unseal the spring of loving kindness."*

---

[10] Sogyal Rinpoche, *Tibetan Book of Living and Dying,* Harper Collins, 1994.

To do that he suggests going back in your mind and recreate, almost visualize, a love that someone gave you that really moved you. My mind wandered through several possibilities both in my adult life and childhood, when suddenly I remembered an instance with my father that was repeated often when I was small ... my father would come to my bed at night when he would get home and playing with my toes.

When I remembered that episode, which had long since been forgotten, I cried because of the love that I was feeling from my father and almost simultaneously a big smile formed on my face. Rinpoche says that, *"You will remember then that even though you may not always feel that you have been loved enough, you were loved genuinely once. Knowing that now will make you feel again that you are, as that person made you feel then, worthy of love and really lovable."* And so it did.

Under his further instruction, I let my heart open and the love that flowed from it was extended to my father, to my family and friends, and to all people. I visualized holding my father as he was dying (I was not there in fact) and saying to him, "You can let go now for I know that you love me and I love you ... I will be ok." I was now ready to practice tonglen on myself.

Rinpoche suggests, for the purpose of this exercise, dividing yourself into two aspects ... one is the aspect of you that is whole, compassionate, etc., the other is the aspect of you that has been hurt, that feels misunderstood, bitter or angry, *"who might have been unjustly treated or abused as a child, or has suffered in relationships or been wronged by society."* As you breathe in, the first aspect opens its heart completely and receives all of the other aspect's pain and suffering. As you breathe out, the first aspect gives the other aspect all its healing love, warmth, trust, and happiness. In response, the other aspect opens its heart to this love and all pain and suffering melt away in this embrace.

What could be more appropriate for me given my history, I thought! And so, I practiced tonglen on myself with beneficial results. Indeed, as the weeks and months passed, I practiced both the visualization of my father's love, as well as tonglen on myself, on a regular basis. Each time I did, I felt that smile ... the smile of happiness and love ... form naturally and for many weeks tears would roll down my cheek. Clearly, this was a very cathartic experience for me.

Our awareness of the truths of samsara also opens the intellectual door to feeling compassion and respect for ourselves. For the first time in our lives, when our ego throws negative words at us ... bad, stupid, unattractive, failure ... we understand that these are words that reflect the judgment of family, peers, or our culture – they do not reflect the real us.

And although I am responsible for my life, at a deeper level I understood that until I broke out of the cycle of samsara by following the path, my ability to choose or reject and to see clearly was a limited one. Free will is in reality not free at all. Whatever we have done that we may feel remorse or regret for, those are things that often were not really within our control to do much otherwise. And so, we come to have the awareness that allows us to have compassion for ourselves, to love ourselves unconditionally.

But compassion does not stop with ourselves. We learn that just as all people are born with the true Buddha nature inside them, all mankind in every corner of the earth, regardless how poor or how rich, regardless whether kind or cruel, regardless whether civilized or not, suffers from samsara. The details may be different in different people, but the experience of samsara is universal.

The awareness of the oneness of all humanity in both its essential purity and its suffering opens the door to having compassion for all people. Even the Rwandan who wielded a machete or the Nazi SS guard who sent thousands to their death or the Charles Mansons of the world ... all of these individuals are deserving of compassion because they are victims of their own samsara. Regarding all one can truly say, "there but for the grace of God go I."[11]

Compassion and respect for all people ... and beyond that, for all sentient beings and the environment ... lies at the heart of Buddhism. It is the rock on which the Five Precepts rest. Every day when I prostrate myself, I invoke the Bodhisattva of Compassion with the Korean words, "Gwanseum bosal," and commit to cultivating a compassionate heart towards myself and all others.

---

[11] Jesus' statement from the cross is also very relevant, "Father forgive them for they know not what they do."

ACCEPTING LIFE

How do we find acceptance for our life, when we've spent our life not accepting it? It's like the old question of the chicken and the egg ... which comes first? Here the question is, is one only able to truly accept ones life as being the way it is right now after realizing the impermanence of all things and the illusory nature of all perceptions, or is acceptance an important initial step that makes it easier to meditate on the truths of impermanence and illusion?

This is not a trivial theoretical question. The answer has significant practical implications for the practitioner.

We are all victims of our cravings, our unskillful desires. While in the grip of those cravings, it is very hard for most people to "wrap their heads" around the concept of the illusory nature of all perceptions. We think we know the world and our condition in it. To not trust our mind, our senses, is a very unsettling proposition. And so, I made little if any progress towards this very important marker on the Buddhist path. My samsara continued unabated.

Even when in the grip of cravings, however, we are still usually capable in calmer moments of being aware of the wonderful things in our life ... be it our family, our job, our hobbies, our friends, the wonders of nature, the warmth of our bed, things large and small, whatever. I don't mean to be glib, but regardless how dissatisfied one is with ones life, there are always aspects that give us joy or that we feel good about when we stop and think about it. That certainly was true for me.

Is there a way of using that awareness to make progress on the path to accepting life? I believe the answer is, yes.

The first step I took was to work with this revealed fact. I focused on the good things in my life without saying, "Yes, but I don't have ... . " I tried to be aware of those things and be grateful for them ... but not attach to them ... throughout the day, especially when I got up in the morning and when I went to bed at night. Writing a short mantra for myself on this subject helped me focus. This is the teaching contained in the previous sections on "Smiling Mindfully" and "Taking Joy in Each Moment."

When you have, if not turned your mind from your cravings, at least given the good things in your life equal time in your mind, then you are ready for the second step ... understanding the difference between skillful and unskillful desires.

One reason why we have a problem with acceptance is our fear of the unknown. "How will I pursue my life if I accept things as they are now?" Even if we understand that acceptance does not mean resignation, we think that acceptance entails letting go of our hopes and dreams. And the idea of that is unacceptable.

But that is not the case. Following the path does not mean letting go of all desires and hopes ... just unskillful ones. What turns an otherwise skillful desire into an unskillful one is often its origin in a lack of equanimity. Your desire may be in keeping with the five Precepts and thus skillful, but if it is based on your running from what is, if you are dissatisfied, then it becomes unskillful; it becomes a craving.

And what causes this lack of equanimity? Why do these hopes and dreams seem so crucial to our being that they create the destructive cravings that bring us only pain and frustration?

Hopes and dreams may be a function of human nature, but the lack of equanimity that transforms them into powerful cravings that cause suffering is caused by something else ... a lack of acceptance of ourselves, of who we are, and a lack of acceptance of our lives. If we do not have compassion for ourselves and love ourselves *unconditionally*, if we want to be something or someone other, we will suffer. If we are so blinded by cravings that we cannot see that we have what we need, what is most important to us,[12] right now, we will suffer. If we do not accept our lives, we will suffer.

So, if following the guidance of the previous section you have accepted yourself, if you love yourself unconditionally and have compassion for yourself, then you are almost there; your equanimity has begun to blossom. To the extent that you truly accept your life as it is right now, your equanimity will be complete and your skillful desires will remain skillful; your cravings and frustration will cease. (I say "to the extent" because at this stage of your practice, it is likely that your deepest insecurities and neuroses will not be capable of being neutralized so easily.)

The other problem people face when contemplating acceptance is that that very statement brings up all the things about their lives or the world around them that they don't like. And so, getting drawn into those negative thoughts, they make no progress with acceptance.

Once again, one answer to this barrier is our understanding that all of our perceptions of our selves and the world around us are labels that we apply based on our learned experience. We may not have reached the point where we truly understand the illusory nature of all perceptions, but we do understand the concept of our labels. And just like the labels we apply to ourselves don't reflect the real us, our true Buddha nature, the labels we apply to the world around us don't reflect the real world

---

[12] And by "what we need" and "important" I mean whatever we experience at the moment that brings us well-being and joy, while realizing that all things are impermanent and not attaching to them. In other words, it's not the specific things we have at the moment, but the awareness that at any moment of any day of any year, there are things we experience that will bring us well-bring and joy ... whether they be things outside or inside of ourselves. Even in our darkest moments when our world may look very bleak, we know that those strengthening experiences are open to us if we are open to them.

either, even though those labels are strongly supported by our culture. When we meditate on that truth, the power of our negative thoughts, our dislikes, will decrease.[13]

Another answer to this barrier lies in the teaching, "it's just the way it is." Once many years ago, I asked a monk why, if we are all born essentially perfect, suffering was such a common human experience. His answer was, "It's just the way it is. It's like the law of thermodynamics."

When I heard his words it was like a huge burden was lifted from my shoulders. While acceptance was still key to achieving peace and serenity, that acceptance was made easier by understanding that things are the way they are because it's just the way they are ... even if something still did have a negative label in my mind. It wasn't really for me to accept; it just was. Similarly, the age-old question, "Why me?" misses the point ... it has nothing to do with "me."[14] Having absorbed the teaching of "it's just the way it is," it was easier for me to accept my life and the world around me.

Once I understood these things and that acceptance does not mean consigning myself to a life in the future that is devoid of hopes and desires, then I was able to take the third step, which is to *truly* accept ... happily ... my life as being the way it is right now. These concepts are synergistic. This is not a mental trick; it is an honest way of resolving a very real obstacle to making progress on the path.

The change this brought about in my life cannot be overstated. As an example, for most of my life, I did not love myself unconditionally or have compassion for myself.

---

[13] The point made in the previous section about what to do if you cannot acknowledge these truths applies here as well.

[14] This is not in conflict with the Buddha's teaching of cause and effect or the Four Noble Truths. The point here is that whether speaking of cosmic forces or personal ones, when you ask the larger question, "Why is this happening?" the answer is that it's just the way it is. There is no intelligent force or God that is orchestrating what happens.

And so I was obsessed with finding companionship, both for security and to feel wanted or loved. The perfectly healthy and skillful desire for friends or loved ones was transformed into a deep craving and frustration. My insecurity and anxiety were so extreme that even when I was in a relationship, I would be so afraid of losing it that my craving and frustration would continue unabated.

But once I began to love myself unconditionally and have compassion, and began to accept my life as it was, knowing that I could still have skillful hopes and dreams, my demons deflated and my desire for companionship returned to its skillful state. I know now that my fear of being alone was just a function of the negative view I had of myself based on learned experience. There is no fear of being alone when you love yourself unconditionally and are at one with all things.

But beware, the line separating skillful and unskillful desires is very thin. It is difficult to both accept oneself and ones life and desire what one does not have; that is why the two are usually thought to be mutually exclusive and all desire is classified as unskillful. Desires have a way of pulling one away from ones acceptance. In order to keep our desires skillful, we must thus be disciplined in the practice of gratitude and acceptance until they are so deeply engrained that they become a paradigm of our life.

One also needs to be aware that because our ego and its cravings are so strong and wily, it is quite possible that when one reads these sections and responds positively to accepting oneself and ones life as it is, that acceptance will be merely an illusion, a self-deception. In that case, nothing will have changed and your cravings will be as strong and destructive as before. That is why I italicized the word "truly" when I wrote, "to *truly* accept my life."

What one needs to do in order to not fall into this trap is to give your acceptance some space and time to take root. This is after all a major shift for us after spending most of our lives not accepting. And we need to recognize that our craving for things is basically an addiction ... we feel we need them to be happy ... and so we need to follow the practice of 12-step programs and commit to not entertaining any of our desires/scravings for a period of time ... however long it takes until you can honestly say that you accept yourself and your life as it is right now.

Your ego will certainly scream at you, "But I want [whatever]!" When it does that, you need to respond that you have what you need right now and you have faith that if you live each day well ... living a life in keeping with the Precepts ... the future will take care of itself. End of story!

Having begun to free ourselves from the twin obstructions of dissatisfaction with our lives and craving what we don't have, we find that we are now able to practice the third Paramita ... patience ... and experience the abiding calm that comes with it.

As regards accepting the state of the world as it is right now, my compassion for all beings together with the teaching of "it's just the way it is" has altered the nature of my interaction with the news of the day and the world at large. No longer do I become angry and agitated. Instead I have concern and compassion.

As you focus on the wonderful things in your life and begin developing unconditional love and compassion for yourself and others, accepting your life as it is now, freeing yourself from unskillful desires, and practicing patience, then you will begin to experience the serenity and peace that is necessary to meditate on the twin truths of impermanence and the illusory nature of all perceptions. However long it may take to realize the emptiness of all five skandhas,[15]

---

[15] The "five skandhas" are generally defined as the five physical and mental elements that comprise the existence of a person: form, feelings, perceptions, mental formations and consciousness. They are also referred to as "aggregates." The skandhas are discussed more fully and

when you reach that state you will be open to surrendering your ego to your true Buddha nature and, as the Heart Sutra teaches, you will be at one with all things, experiencing things directly without the intervention of thought, thus ending doubt and suffering.

---

the definition tweaked and differentiated in Chapter 4 of my book, *The Self in No Self: Buddhist Heresies and Other Lessons of a Buddhist Life*

STAYING GROUNDED

Once I achieved a platform of serenity, the challenge was then to maintain it. In addition to continuing doing the things that brought me serenity as part of a disciplined daily practice, there was one more necessary element ... staying grounded.

As I make my way through life, there were and will likely continue to be many challenges to my Buddhist practice and my serenity. I have found that this is especially true of anything that I put energy and effort into.

Until we reach a state of enlightenment, even if we have surrendered our ego to our true Buddha nature[16] and are in general at peace and content, feel at one with all things, are free of labels and attachments, and truly accept our life as it is, when we put effort into an activity, our ego often arises, looking to be stroked. And if it is not stroked, we get frustrated. (Of course if we haven't surrendered our ego, etc., the likelihood of our ego arising is almost a certainty.)

Even if your desires are Right desires in that they are of skillful origination and in keeping with the Precepts and your efforts are self-less, ego still seems to arise when we are investing ourselves in some activity. Since putting forth effort is an integral part of living and indeed of Right effort, is there an answer to this conundrum?

Your initial reaction may be ... "Ah, this is a sign that I've been deceiving myself; I'm not truly accepting of my life or I'm not being truly self-less." While that may of course be true, it is not necessarily so.

It is an inherent part of human nature that when we put forth effort, we do it for a reason, for an end ... for

---

[16] For more on surrendering your ego, see the chapter, "The Last Barrier – Surrendering the Ego: The Missing Noble Truth," in my book, *The Self in No Self: Buddhist Heresies and Other Lessons of a Buddhist Life*.

example, to help others, to further our career, to resolve a problem, or just to learn or create something ... otherwise we would not put forth the effort to begin with. (NOTE: If you are doing such an activity because you feel the need to fix an inadequacy you feel, to "improve" yourself, then the activity is not skillful because it stems from a lack of equanimity that needs to be addressed.) And so, even if we truly accept our life, our ego often attaches unseen to such effort.

We learn that in pursuing a plan we should be present in the moment, not to attach, and not think about the future, about the outcome, but what if the present moment is a setback to our skillful effort? If we are not attached to our effort, we will say that it's just the way it is; the world will continue to move forward. It will not frustrate us. But if we have not been mindful and our ego arises and attaches to the effort, we will be frustrated.

For those efforts where, once we have produced something, we are dependent on others for its acceptance/use, a different dynamic often occurs. Rather than letting it go at that point, not thinking about the future, we often find ourselves consumed by doubt and desire during the seemingly eternal process of waiting for feedback and check our email or phone messages constantly for some word. This is very demoralizing and robs us of our peace. Without question, we have not been mindful and our ego has attached to the effort.

The solution to this inescapable conundrum is to stay grounded. Whether it's your job, your volunteer work, or a book you're trying to write or market, you must make sure that the task does not consume you and rob you of your peace.

How we stay grounded depends on how far along you are with your practice. If you are at the point where you have developed the practice of being mindful and of nonattachment, then the answer is certainly to be mindful, to be aware when the ego arises, and to confirm your nonattachment to the activity.

But if you are not at that point in your practice, you can stay grounded by first being present, which will allow you to be aware of the things and people that bring you joy, know that you have what you need, what is important to you right now, and maintain your focus in life on those things, as well as being disciplined in your practice of acceptance, compassion, loving yourself unconditionally, and meditation.

The key is to see your frustration or anger as a red flag ... it is your canary in a mine ... that one of two things is happening: either you are engaged in an activity or pursuing a goal which is not healthy for you, not consistent with the Five Precepts, or the activity or goal is in the abstract a healthy, skillful one, but you are approaching it in an unhealthy way, for example it is a craving that stems from a lack of equanimity.

When you experience frustration or anger, the first thing you must do is stop. Without stopping you cannot apply your spirituality to the situation. Center yourself by watching your breathing, using a technique as suggested in previous section on aware breath.

To determine whether the activity is just an ego trip or otherwise unhealthy, first ask yourself whether the activity is consistent with the Five Precepts. If it is, then ask, "Could this effort realistically make a difference?" The more macro the effort, the more likely that the answer to this question may be a painful, no. If it is either inconsistent with the Five Precepts or just an extension of your ego, then you need to drop the project to regain your sense of peace and contentment.

But if your effort really could make a difference, whether in one person's life or many, but the problem is that you are approaching it from a lack of equanimity, then ... since the assumption here is that you have not yet reached the state of practice where you are able to practice nonattachment ... you need to find a way to approach the activity in a healthy, non-craving way.

For most types of efforts you will help yourself stay grounded by limiting your time exposure to the activity. Keep your commitment appropriate with your focus on the things that bring you joy, that give you strength, and thus limit any potential negative impact.

You can't do that with your job, of course. Especially in today's work environment when there is often pressure to work almost 24/7. But even here, you must not only carve out time for your family and other things that bring you joy ... those things must psychologically be the center of your life, not your work. It is a sad statement of our culture that for many people work has become their life; they live to work, not work to live.

A helpful compliment to maintaining the right focus in your life is to remember the teaching ... it's just the way it is ... and meditate on that truth. Whatever is bothering you about the effort you are making, it's just the way it is.

It's also helpful to remember that we have no control over the future and can have no idea what is going to transpire ... therefore why obsess about what will happen? It's a no-win situation that robs you of your peace in the present, which is where you really need it. Instead, have faith that if you live each day well, in keeping with the five Precepts, the future will take care of itself ... although not necessarily in the way you have planned.

Another tool that helps keep things in perspective is to engage in activities that relax you, calm you (beyond the spiritual ones already noted in this chapter). As adults, most of us have a real deficit in this area. Even activities that we supposedly do to relax us, to get away from things ... like playing golf, playing an instrument, shopping, whatever ... do not relax us because our ego is involved in those activities. They may be a distraction, but they are not calming.

What you need to do is some activity that puts you in touch with your inner child, that innocent being who was and is still free from the burdens of life and most learned experience. Most adults in our culture are closed off to their inner child; somehow it's not felt appropriate for adults to engage in childlike behavior or activities. And yet those activities, and the simple laughter that often accompanies them, give one access to the well of innocent joy that only a child experiences. Whether you used to love coloring books, climbing trees, playing with your dog (this is not to be confused with what adults do with their dogs in a dog park), or whatever, allow yourself the simple joy of immersing yourself in such activities with some regularity.

There is a deeper answer, however, to the question of how to stay grounded. There is a line in the classic Chinese poem, *Affirming Faith in Mind*, that says, "When the mind rests undisturbed then nothing in the world offends. And when no thing can give offense, then all obstructions cease to be."[17]

We are frustrated in these situations because our ego takes offense when we are not stroked. And the ego takes offense because these situations disturb our mind and our ego arises.

Why do these situations disturb our mind? Because we do not experience them free of labels, free of our past. For most of us these situations touch the deepest insecurities from our childhood about who we are, how we are valued, and whether we are liked or loved. Whenever we put ourselves, our talent, our credibility on the line, this ego insecurity is awakened.

And so the deeper, more fundamental, solution to such frustration is to meditate on the truth that fear, guilt, and

---

[17] Roshi Phillip Kapleau, op. cit.

shame are learned. We must free ourselves from othe past. Whatever made us feel insecure as children, that emotional reaction was a learned experience and does not reflect who we really were; it was a cultural or family judgment. And those judgments do not speak the truth; they are biased. Our cultural obsession with "improving" ourselves is not founded on a desire to learn more or do other things, it is based on a perception that we are inadequate in some way, that we are failures, and that that needs to be fixed. But we are not inadequate; we are not failures. These perceptions of ours have no intrinsic value; they are all of dependent origination.

And so, being free of these perceptions and feelings or at least aware of their nature, we meditate on being at one with ourselves, experiencing ourselves without the intervention of thought. And we meditate on loving ourselves unconditionally, finding peace and hope in the present.

As noted above, even if you are at the point in your practice where you've surrendered your ego to your true Buddha nature, this can still happen; the ego can still arise. "How can that be?" you may ask. The ego does not disappear; it does not vanish from our existence; it remains part of us. It may no longer factor into our view of the world and our everyday lives ... but when our innermost insecurities are touched it can arise and regain a foothold in our mind. That is why we must be as mindful as we can, be aware when the ego arises, and confirm our nonattachment if we have reached that point in our practice or otherwise just say to our ego, as noted earlier, that we have chosen a different path.

Free At Last

When I was a young man
I was consumed by a silent anger
Against the world and our culture.

I felt unwanted and unloved,
At times even despised, by others.
I could not accept the world as being
Just the way it is
Because I felt unfairly rejected by the world.
Feeling rejected,
I perversely rejected myself,
Believing what I was taught by the world.
And rejecting myself
Enflamed my anger all the more.

But when I found the Buddha dharma
I learned that I and all others were born
Essentially perfect
With the true Buddha nature
That remains intact throughout our lives.
The things that I had learned about myself,
All the labels, were false.
When I understood that my perceptions of
Myself were a product of the world
And not a product of who I was,
I was freed of these perceptions,
I believed in my true Buddha nature.
And when I believed in my true Buddha nature
I was able to love myself unconditionally and
Have compassion for myself;
I was able to accept myself just as I was.
And when I accepted myself just as I was
I was able to accept the world as being
Just the way it is
And have compassion for all people.
And when I accepted the world as it is
And found compassion for all people
I was freed from anger.
I felt sorrow and concern,
But I was free at last

Chapter 2
How Does a Buddhist Think About the Future?

We all know that the Buddhist maxim is to live life in the present. There are few principles more critical to walking the Buddhist path. If we are not able to be present we are lost in the maze of our ego-mind, worrying about the future and the past, a captive of our samsara.

We also know that one cannot live life, at least as a layperson, without some amount of planning, which means thinking about the future. Whether it's deciding what kind of work or career to pursue, or what kind of garden to plant, or what school to send our children to, or countless other decisions, including even following the path, planning/thinking about the future is an inescapable part of a layperson's life.

And all these things we plan for are personal desires. Yet aren't desires the same as cravings, the root of our suffering?

Thus the following conundrums: how to live life as a Buddhist when it comes to planning. How can one reconcile the teaching of being in the present and the life-function of planning? How can one have desires and not be caught in a web of cravings?

HOW TO PLAN YET REMAIN PRESENT

Although what I have to say on this subject is pretty straightforward and short, it deserves separate treatment because it is a central problem for anyone trying to live as a Buddhist, affecting all areas of our life. Wondering how to be both present and plan brings frequent frustration for most of us.

Although one cannot make any kind of plans for the future without thinking about the future, making that decision should be done with as much equanimity as you can muster and as free of your ego as your awareness will allow. To do this, you must bring your mindfulness to bear on the process. This is a critical point ... to the extent that your decision is made from a lack of equanimity and with your ego fully involved, it will be that much harder if not impossible to not attach to it and stay present.

Once you have made your decision, hopefully mindfully, and obtain knowledge regarding the steps that you will need to take to attain your goal, you must let go all thoughts of the future and live your life in the present. That is the simple answer to this conundrum.

As you live each day well in conformity with the Five Precepts, some days will contain activities that pertain to your plans, but think of them only in the present. Do the work you know you have to do in a disciplined and mindful way; the only thing you should be concerned about is making the best effort you are capable of today. What you cannot do is think about let alone obsess about the future, about whether your efforts will be successful in meeting your goals.

Our lives need direction. But it is important to remember while saying that that we know that we have no control over the future, so although we may plan as carefully as we can, and do everything by the book, what will be will be. Being aware of that and accepting that basic fact is one of the keys to staying present while planning. Why obsess over something over which we have no control and thereby rob us of peace in the present? That's hard for our ego to accept, but that's just the way it is.

Without question this is easier said than done. As discussed earlier in the section on "Staying Grounded," our ego tends to arise whenever we put our effort into something, regardless of its nature, and we easily fall into the trap of obsessing about the future. All the suggestions made in that section are of value in helping to keep you present.

But bottom line, the key to planning without the frustration that comes from not living in the present is to not attach to your plans and to be mindful, to catch yourself whenever your mind starts to fantasize or obsess about the future or to worry about whether your current efforts will be successful in bringing you to the point you have planned. As suggested earlier, use your frustration as a red flag ... your canary in the mine ... to help you stop and catch yourself.

Again, once you have made your decision about your future goal, you must mindfully let go any thought of it and just do the best you can each day, knowing that whether it comes to pass or not, your life will go on just fine. This is what it means to not be attached.

Depending on what stage you are at with your practice, this lesson will be easier or harder to follow. But even if you have not yet the mindfulness to catch yourself or the true acceptance to be free of attachment to your plans, keeping this lesson in mind, being aware of these things, while maintaining your focus on the things that bring you joy right now, in the present, will make your life more free of frustration.

As with all aspects of the Buddhist path, finding this freedom is incremental. Better to have some awareness and freedom from frustration, than no awareness and constant turmoil. Have faith that if you live each day well, the future *will* take care of itself.

HOW TO DESIRE YET NOT CRAVE

The Buddha taught that craving is one of the afflictions that cause us suffering. This thought has been touched on earlier in this book ... to crave what one does not have can be the result of illusory perceptions, a mistaken concept of permanence, and perhaps most importantly not accepting our lives as being the way they are now and were in the past. It has certainly been a major cause of my suffering. At the root of craving is desire.

The reader may have noticed that I have referred to such desires that become cravings as "unskillful desires," thereby implying that there is such a thing as a "skillful desire." Yet the concept of a skillful desire, a Right desire is not found in traditional Buddhist teaching. Typically, the two words ... desire and craving ... are equated, even though in Pali as in English, they are two separate words with different meanings.

Several years ago, however, I happened to hear a series of dharma talks on tape given by a learned student of the Buddha dharma on this very topic.[18] It made sense to me, it fit with the dharma, and I felt it was very helpful in making ones way along the path. And so, I want to share my understanding of that teaching with you.

As a Buddhist, the five Precepts ... not killing, helping others, refraining from sexual misconduct, speaking and listening with loving kindness, and not consuming things which are harmful ... are an essential element of ones meditation practice and form a core guidance on how to live a Right life. We know that vast numbers of people on this earth do not follow these precepts, and not only do they suffer for it, but those who they abuse suffer as well. Indeed, most of us can point to many moments in our own

---

[18] Larry Yang, San Francisco, CA.

past and even occasions in the present when we did not act in accordance with the Precepts.

Can one, as a Buddhist, "desire" to address this source of suffering, both by directly helping those in need and by spreading the Buddha dharma and bringing the benefits of its teaching to more people? Can we desire, for ourselves and others, a life that is in keeping with the Precepts? What about work ... can we not desire to help others through our work, in ways both large and small? In general, can we desire things that are consistent with the Five Precepts? Is this not what engaged Buddhism is about?

It was with much surprise that I recently found that the Buddha as well as Larry Yang would say, "yes." Listen to what the Buddha said:

> *What is right effort?* Here a bhikkhu awakens desire for the non-arising of ... unwholesome states, the abandoning of arisen unwholesome states, the arising of wholesome states, and the perfecting of arisen wholesome states, for which he makes efforts, arouses energy, exerts his mind, and endeavors.[19]

If that is not support for the concept of Right desire and engaged Buddhism, I don't know what is.

However, the teaching I received on skillful v unskillful desires notes one major caveat. And that caveat is that if such a desire has an unskillful origination either because of intent or lack of equanimity, then the desire is unskillful and a craving (or to use the Buddha's phrasing, an unwholesome state).

Let me give some examples. Desiring to help others is a skillful desire, but if that desire arises from the intent to create an image of oneself as being good, then the desire becomes unskillful. Indeed the unskillful intent in this case indicates that one is not really interested in helping others.

---

[19] Bhikkhu Nanamoli, *The Life of the Buddha*, BPS Pariyatti Editions, 1992, p.239

Desiring to have friends is a skillful desire, but if that desire arises from dissatisfaction with ones life as it is now, if one is running from what is ... from loneliness ... then the desire becomes unskillful; it arises from a lack of equanimity. Whereas, if one is content with ones life as it is now, accepts that it's just the way it is, and desires to have friends, then the desire is skillful.

Desiring to have a sexual relationship in a physically and psychologically healthy way is a skillful desire. But if that desire becomes obsessive, then the desire becomes unskillful because it arises from a lack of equanimity.

So, desires that are in furtherance of, or in keeping with, the five Precepts *and* are not tainted by unskillful origination are Right desires. They can and indeed should be acted upon for they move us along the path, they increase our happiness; they are skillful.

But beware that your ego does not play tricks on you. It is critically important to be mindful of the arising of desire and to be aware of its origination. To ensure that one's desires remain or become Right desires, it is essential that you *truly* accept your life as it is now. If our acceptance is self-deception, our desires will remain cravings. Thus, as explained more fully in the earlier section on "Acceptance," because the ego and cravings are so strong we need to give our acceptance an opportunity to take root before we engage in any desires, even potentially skillful ones.

There is yet one more caveat. As explained more fully in the earlier section, "Staying Grounded," the mere fact that you are putting effort and energy into something causes the ego to arise, looking to be stroked. This destroys your equanimity and the desire becomes unskillful.

To stay grounded and keep the desire skillful, we should both keep our primary focus on the people and/or things that bring us joy and meditate on loving ourselves unconditionally, acceptance, and the truth that "it's just the way it is."

Now someone might say that despite the fact that Bhikkhu Nanamoli translated Right Effort using the word "desire," such "good" desires are not desires at all ... a desire is something obsessive, it controls our life, it by definition causes suffering. Certainly most desires, wants, cravings fit that definition. But I would counter that a desire is simply wanting something that is not. So while the skillful desire I have defined is not harmful, it is nevertheless a desire. Indeed, if one is far along in ones practice and is free of ego, such a desire can result directly from ones true Buddha nature rather than be the result of a choice one makes.

Desire is not in and of itself a harmful thing. It is the nature of a specific desire and its origination that renders it a harmful craving rather than Right.

Chapter 3
Personal Life

Love ... family ... personal relationships ... these sound as though they should be respites from the dog eat dog atmosphere of the typical workplace and the broader world. And while that was to a large extent true for me, these personal fronts posed their own stresses to my psyche, which were even worse because they went to the core of my insecurities that had developed as a child. I only came to Buddhism when I was 49, so I did not have the benefit of what I know now during the more active phase of my personal life. While from the outside my life looked very successful, both professionally and personally, inside my life was very troubled and in pretty constant turmoil. Thankfully, with the awareness I have gained on the Buddhist path as my practice has deepened, my personal life this past decade has been filled with ever more peace, contentment, joy, and happiness

. . . .

HOW TO LOVE

Remember I said this was going to be difficult? Well, here goes.

In many ways, the most challenging relationships from a Buddhist perspective are the relationships with those you love ... especially your spouse or significant other. The reason is that everything we know about love comes from the culture we live in, and that learned information and experience is not usually conducive to a truly healthy relationship.

If this sounds a bit over the top, think about these facts. Roughly 50% of marriages end in divorce. A whole industry has grown up around marital counseling. Spouse abuse is not uncommon. There is no end to the problems, whether acknowledged or not, in many marriages between two people who supposedly at least at one point in time loved each other.

But did they really love each other? Krishnamurti says that you can only truly love someone if you do not need that person.[20] Otherwise, what you really love is what that person does for you, not the person. It is not surprising then that as needs and people change, people find themselves drifting apart and the feeling of love dissolves because their needs are no longer being met within the relationship. The result is a high divorce rate, now that divorce is available and carries little social stigma, if any.

Where do we get our ideas of what love is? When it comes to role models, many can't look to their parents because their relationship was fraught with problems, had little warmth, and showed clear signs of strain. There just didn't seem to be much love there. Certainly not the type of romantic love that, with periodic exceptions, has been promoted by our culture as the picture of true love and which therefore has affected what we expect and desire from love.

But what we see portrayed in films and books often has little to do with real life. Whether it's how love develops … rarely should we expect to be swept off our feet … or its day-to-day operation … it is far more complex than portrayed … the media version of love has created unrealistic expectations in many people.[21] While romance may be a part of the experience, it does not define love.

---

[20] J. Krishnamurti, *Freedom From the Known*, HarperSanFrancisco, 1969
[21] Andrew Sullivan, "The Way We Live Now: The Love Bloat," New York Times Magazine, February 11, 2001

I once had my own brush with this phenomenon. I had been dating someone and it was going very nicely. Then one evening when we were out to dinner, I was told that it wasn't going to work because when I opened the door the first time, his reaction wasn't, "Yes, that's the one!" In between his sobs I was told, "I know this means I will probably spend my life alone, but I won't settle for anything less than romantic love." How silly. What a waste.

Most of us deal with the dissonance between this image of love and reality by defining love practically as someone who makes us feel good, who meets our needs. But from Krishnamurti's perspective, as noted above, this certainly does not define love. And then there's the inevitable conflict between the fantasy image we retain in our mind and our practically-defined reality. If this approach were successful in terms of nourishing a long-term relationship filled with peace and happiness, one could well say, "So what!" But the proof that it is not successful lies in the data, supported by our own personal experiences ... both as to our lives and those we observe around us.

This leaves open the question, "What is love?" One can dissect it into its elements ... trust, respect, compassion, fondness, caring, sexual attraction, etc. ... but it is more than the sum of its parts. It is a feeling that you would do anything within your power to remove all pain and suffering from your loved one's life. It is the smile that is brought to your face every time you see your loved one. It is a warmth and tenderness that is unconditional.

How can one realistically meet the goal of love as defined by Krishnamurti? If the goal is to love someone for who that person is, not for how that person meets your needs, that either means having no needs, which in turn means being at one with your true Buddha nature, having surrendered your ego and freed yourself from your known/learned experience, or it means being able to see beyond ones needs. Since this book assumes that we are not enlightened or even at a stage in our practice close to enlightenment, the former option is not quite within our reach. So I will briefly discuss how to see beyond your needs.

The key is to accept oneself and one's life as being the way it is right now and thus change our cravings to skillful desires, as discussed earlier in this book. That will enable us to be more aware of our needs and how they influence us, so that when we are developing a relationship or are in one, we can look past the need-fulfilling attributes of a person to who the person really is. One exercise you can do to help with this process is to write down what your needs are in the relationship, and then describe the other attributes the person has that draw you to that person. If there's not much beyond your needs, then you know there is a problem.

By this brief statement, I am not suggesting that this is easy. Far from it; it requires great discipline and steadfastness.

Having said all this, I must admit that during the period of time prior to my finding Buddhism when I was in my longest-term relationship (12 years), I was certainly not at a spiritual place where I accepted myself as I was, although in some respects I accepted my life. And lord knows I had needs, cravings ... a whole panoply of unskillful desires. Nevertheless, I can honestly say that I loved my partner for who he was.

Yes, of course he satisfied many important needs of mine, but there is no question in my mind that my love, which ran very deep, was totally a function of who he was. And the relationship ended only because he died. So it is possible, even with all the baggage I had, to love someone for who that person is.

I don't know how I managed it ... perhaps it was the example of my parents who I believe truly loved each other for who they were, not for how needs were satisfied, which in at least one important way was not the case. Maybe it was evidence of my true Buddha nature before I knew there was such a thing. I just know that I am grateful for that experience.

But what if you are in a relationship where love, regardless how defined, seems to have disappeared. What do you do? The answer is not to hop into bed! Although many might think that renewed sexual ardor will solve relationship problems, it won't. It may make you and your partner feel better, but it won't solve any underlying problems, even if lack of sexual attraction is one of them. One could of course go to a counseling service that helps couples find their love again, however defined.

I would, however, suggest a different approach … one more in keeping with your walking the Buddhist path. When relationships go bad, there usually has been a lot of water that has gone over the proverbial dam. Not only do people say unkind things to one another in moments of despair or anger, but people change and become less responsive. Often people have the reaction, "Where is the person I married?"

The answer without question is that that person is still there; one's true nature does not change over time. It's just that with the passage of time and events various things happen. Your needs often change. All the things that have annoyed you over the years accumulate. Both of your egos have created a layer of veneer, a shell, which acts as a mask to the outside world and barrier to ones own inner feelings. And of course time changes one physically.

The first thing to do is wipe the slate clean so you can approach each other fresh, without any baggage. One cannot seek to reconnect with the weight of all that has happened in the intervening years on your backs, because the ego will constantly bring this history up. This will require great discipline on both of your parts, but it is possible if you understand the following points.

What are the kinds of things that often come between a couple over the years? One is just the process of aging ... our bodies change and sometime people lose sexual interest in a body that has aged. Men often complain that their wives have no time for them, pay no attention to them, have no energy for sex, etc. Women often complain that their husbands are totally absorbed with work, that they hardly relate to them and the kids, and that when they are at home rather than reconnect with wife and family, they replace their work fixation with either the television of some hobby. The same things happen in same sex relationships.

First, the aging process. People's bodies change in all sorts of ways, some of which one can have control over, some not. One owes it to oneself and ones partner to stay healthy and in reasonable shape. It's important not just for your health and but equally important for your energy. This is not to say one should be obsessive about it ... this is not about creating a new craving. It is just about creating a habit energy that involves taking care of oneself. If you haven't been you should commit yourself to starting now; it's never too late.

But there are physical changes that one has no control over, that are an inescapable part of aging. As a Buddhist you should respect that all things are impermanent and changeable. And you should cherish the changes as you age, both in yourself and in your partner. It's about maturing; the old saying that sex is like wine, it improves with aging, is true if approached without any youth hang-ups.

In any relationship, whether it be heterosexual or same-sex, each partner has a role in the relationship and will be quite absorbed in that role ... whether it's making money or being a mother or homemaker. You need to be sufficiently adult to understand this and to not take the involvement of your partner as a rejection or lack of interest in you. What is critical is that each partner respects the other's role and that each understand the need to make time to spend quality time together. I know this sounds like a "duh" statement, but for many couples it just doesn't happen, mostly because our ego is absolute and doesn't care why it doesn't get the attention it wants.

After years or decades of not following this approach and becoming increasingly resentful or distant because of the lack of attention, each person will need to make a real commitment to reconnecting. It will take more than just going on a date to a nice place for dinner one night. It means an attitudinal and functional change in how you relate. And it means communicating with loving kindness and deep listening ... the Fourth Precept.

But how you love is not the only challenge to having a healthy love relationship. There is another aspect of love that needs to be discussed in the context of living life as a Buddhist ... the confluence of love and pain. The Buddha said, "Dear ones who endear themselves bring sorrow and lamentation, pain, grief, and despair."[22]

While that may strike one as an overly negative, one-sided formulation, certainly we have all experienced such suffering ... certainly I have. And as with all suffering, the Buddha dharma shows us the path to be free of it ... how to love without suffering.

Part of the answer to not feeling such suffering is to not be attached to dear ones. (I use the plural because this applies not only to your spouse or significant other, but to your relationship with your children and parents). If that sounds like an inherent contradiction, it is not. One can love someone and yet not be attached to them in the Buddhist sense. Just like love does not imply a co-dependent relationship. This is much easier if you love someone for who the person is rather than their ability to fulfill your needs.

---

[22] Bhikkhu Nanamoli, op. cit., p.96

Of course, even if you are not attached to your loved ones, if your joy comes from their joy, then surely their pain must be felt by you as well. This is inescapable. Regardless the nature of the pain, whether it is physical or psychological, to see a dear one in agony will bring you pain as well.

But the experience of pain does not necessarily lead to suffering. The pain that is a reaction to a stimulus that involves no thought is simple pain. There is no way to not feel it, just as there is no way to not feel pain when you cut yourself. But if there is thought involved in your pain, then what you experience is suffering.

When you feel pain at the pain of a dear one, observe whether it is partly or largely because of the impact that pain or its consequences may have on you in a practical sense, rather than just that the person is in pain. If you think about losing your loved one from illness or otherwise, does it cause you anxiety?

In both cases, a "yes" answer indicates both that you are attached to the person and that you have not grasped one of the centralities of the Buddha dharma ... that all things that arise eventually fall and so it is with love as with birth and death.

When my partner died, I let out a scream that sounded like a hot iron had been pressed into my soul. I certainly experienced and had been experiencing my partner's pain, and in the two years of his illness and with my awareness of so many young men dying of AIDS I was certainly aware of the impermanence of life, but there's no question that I was attached and I think despite my awareness I was at a deeper level in denial about the possibility of his death. I couldn't imagine my life without him. And indeed, virtually my first question to my best friend was, "What am I going to do with my life; how will I fill this void?" And so I not only experienced pain, I suffered. I not only grieved for him; I grieved for me.

To release our attachment and end our anxiety, we must meditate on the impermanence of all things and the illusory nature of our perceptions. The more we are aware of and understand these essential truths the freer we will be from attachments and anxiety. Only then can we love without suffering.

SEX

There's a reason why the expression is, "to lose oneself in the throes of passion," rather than, "to express love or affection through the throes of passion." It's not just that the former is more descriptive of how most of us approach sex, it describes the basic problem in how we approach sex. While sex is a natural ingredient of a healthy life and relationship, it all too often is a key ingredient of an unhealthy life and relationship. What turns sex into one or the other?

The answer is, lust. Lust is one of the main factors identified by the Buddha as causing suffering. Lust is a craving that has at its source a lack of equanimity, and certainly most of us, if we are honest, will admit that our sexual attractions and activities often derive from our insecurity, which is a lack of equanimity.

Many will counter that sex without lust is a boring, mechanical concept ... but that's not what I'm suggesting here. Remember, as discussed earlier, it's not about not having desire, it's about not having unskillful desires or cravings. Many will also defensively argue that sex is a biological necessity, a natural urge. While this is of course true, *when* one chooses to act on that urge is not a biological necessity, at least for humans. Instead, it is more often a psychological imperative.

For many people, sex is a form of validation to escape feelings of insecurity. For men, sex is often a way to project power ... indeed that is its evolutionary biological basis ... and yet the classic comic line, "How was it?" shows that for humans at least, behind the macho surface of the sex act is a deep sense of insecurity. For women, sex is often viewed as a tool to attract and keep a man. Again, while this has its basis in evolutionary biology, it also in humans is evidence of a basic insecurity.

The result of this craving is that there is much sexual misconduct in the world, which leads to unhealthy lives and troubled relationships. Thus, the Third Precept states in its simplest form, "Refrain from sexual misconduct." But that begs the question of what is sexual misconduct.

Some say it is defined by ones culture. While that may be true in a practical or legal sense, I would disagree with that from a spiritual perspective because there have been and are cultures that condone or even encourage sexual activity which is harmful, at least psychologically, to the participants.

If you ask how Buddhists define sexual misconduct, that is not of much help either. All would agree that rape, sexual harassment, and molestation of children are sexual misconduct. But beyond that, the range of behaviors defined as sexual misconduct varies greatly.

At one end of the spectrum, I once asked a Theravadan monk what constitutes sexual misconduct and he said that as long as it was between consenting adults, sex was ok and there was no misconduct. At the other end of the spectrum is Thich Nhat Hanh, who has interpreted the Third Precept as follows:

> "Aware of the suffering caused by sexual misconduct, I am committed to cultivating responsibility and learning ways to protect the safety and integrity of individuals, couples, families, and society. I am determined not to engage in sexual relations without love and a long-term commitment. To preserve the happiness of myself and others, I am determined to respect my commitments and the commitments of others."[23]

---

[23] Thich Nhat Hanh, *The Heart of the Buddha's Teaching*, Broadway Books, 1998, p.95

Further confusing the issue is that while the language that is typically used to define sexual misconduct does not make any reference to and therefore does not differentiate between heterosexual and homosexual conduct, the Dalai Lama for one has commented that homosexual sex is sexual misconduct, based apparently on Tibetan Buddhism's prohibition on the use of anything other than the heterosexual sex-organs for sex. For the other Buddhist traditions, however, homosexual conduct is not, in and of itself, misconduct; it is viewed the same way that heterosexual conduct is viewed.

Since this is a practical guide, the rest of this discussion will first deal with sex and the single person, and then deal with sex and the married/long-term committed person.

The first important thing to note for the single person is that there is no proscription in Buddhism regarding premarital sex. Even Thich Nhat Hanh talks about a "loving, long-term commitment," which does not necessarily imply marriage.

In our culture, it is not unusual for single men, and increasingly single women, to seek consensual sexual relationships that include:

- the very casual ... that is, one barely knows the other person;
- "friends with benefits"
- sex with various partners during the same period of time
- sex within a dating situation, and
- sex within a short-term committed relationship

In helping us navigate this question, it is most important to remember that the primary Buddhist moral principles are to treat others with respect and loving kindness and to do others no harm, psychologically or physically. These will be our guiding principles.

If we look at these various situations from this perspective, I would argue that casual sex, friends with benefits, and sex with various partners are all in the Buddhist context, misconduct. While one can be kind in each of these situations, one cannot act with loving kindness because typically one is acting from a lack of equanimity. While the situations are indeed consensual, one or both partners are using the other to fill a craving and thus some level of suffering is inevitable. Such free love is never really free. As a Buddhist, you should not engage in such sex.

As to sex in a dating situation or in a short-term committed relationship, the question that you must ask yourself is whether the sex is based on a craving, that is a lack of equanimity based on insecurity, or whether the sex flows from your feelings of love or affection or fondness for the other person. If the latter, it is not misconduct; if the former, it is.

To answer this question, one must look deep inside oneself in meditation and be very aware and honest. If the answer is that the sex is based on a lack of equanimity, then not only should you not have sex with this person, you also need to meditate on the issue of sexual craving so that you are able to have healthy sexual relations in the future.

Ideally you would come to the understanding that your insecurities are all based on your learned experience; they are illusory; they are not based on reality. When you realize that your thoughts and feelings have no intrinsic existence, you would surrender your ego to your true Buddha nature, be one with your true Buddha nature and your lack of equanimity would be a thing of the past.

But again, since the premise of this book is that we are not enlightened, what to do if your meditation does not bring you to this point? As stated earlier, the key is to accept oneself and one's life as being the way it is right now and thus change our desires from cravings to skillful desires. That will enable us to be more aware of our needs and approach the prospect of sex from a place of at least greater equanimity.

If you are able to be very mindful of the dynamics of your relationship and constantly remind yourself to think of your partner and not of yourself, you can approximate a caring relationship filled with loving kindness. But if you cannot do this, if you continue to approach sex out of insecurity and craving and only care for your partner because of what that person can do for you, then you cannot treat the person with loving kindness let alone really love someone. Until you master the art of loving/caring and can approach sex with equanimity, you should thus not engage is sexual relations, since that would be sexual misconduct under the standards I have set. This probably sounds harsh, but if you are not able to approach sex other than as a craving, then you will only harm yourself and the other person.

What about sex in a married or a long-term committed relationship? That status does not automatically make sex with your spouse/significant other ok.

"Oh, come on!" the reader may say. Many will find it a stretch to describe sex in such a relationship, even if it stems from a lack of equanimity and is not based on loving kindness, as being sexual misconduct. One of the reasons, after all, why many people got married in the past was so that they could have morally-blessed sex.

But as I have defined the parameters, sex without skillful origination in such a relationship is nevertheless misconduct, in the sense of the Third Precept. Marriage or a long-term commitment does not make your spouse/significant other an available sex object. If sex does not flow from your love or affection but from a lack of equanimity, then you are not treating your spouse/significant other with respect and are potentially causing that person hurt.

In former times, sex in marriages was often both loveless and unskillful (in the technical sense). There was no pleasure in it, certainly not for the woman. Now, sex is more often characterized by technical skill and pleasure and lust, but loveless sex is probably no less common.

As a Buddhist, if you are married or in a long-term committed relationship and fall into this category of loveless sex, the need to resolve this problematic state through meditation, the suggestions made in the previous section, and possibly some type of counseling, is even more compelling. The alternative of continuing in this state is harmful to both you and your partner and should not be acceptable, and the alternative of divorce/separation is wrenching, especially if there are any children involved.

There are many who would say that if there are children, the couple should stay together, almost no matter what. I would disagree. Children deserve and need a loving, stable environment. If they are living in an environment that is not loving and stable, their learned experience will be very negative and their psychological development harmed.

But whether you have children or not, ultimately, if you're not in a relationship for the right reasons, and meditation or counseling does not resolve the problems and create the basis for a good relationship, then you need to get out of it. That is the only truly fair course of action.

There is another issue presented in the situation where one is married or in a long-term committed relationship ... and that is sex outside the relationship. Here I would agree with Thich Nhat Hanh that no matter how consensual, no matter how loving the outside relationship is, adultery is sexual misconduct for it shows no respect for one's spouse and no respect for the commitment you have made. Such sex cannot be viewed in any way other than being hurtful to ones spouse.

If one feels so out of love that one desires, indeed must have, a sexual liaison whether casual or as a relationship outside your commitment, then you should get a divorce. Some may argue that they do love their spouse; they're just sexually bored.

I'm sorry, but if you truly love your spouse, you would not be sexually bored. But even granting that premise for argument's sake, that's no excuse. Indeed, especially *if* you truly love your spouse, hurting him or her (and also any children you may have) in this way should be totally unacceptable to you. This is a perfect example of ones ego running away with one, clouding all reason other than what it wants. Again, if you find yourself in this situation you must meditate on acceptance as noted above.

If your craving is totally out of control because you are a sex addict, then you have a more difficult problem and need to seek help, whether from a 12-step program or otherwise. You and your partner will need to discuss this openly and you will need your partner's support if the relationship is to continue.

The key in this situation is having the awareness and knowledge to identify oneself as a sex addict. As a grateful recovering sex and love addict, I can attest to that. Back in the 70s when I became an addict, promiscuous sex was so commonplace in the gay community, regardless whether one was in a relationship (monogamy was viewed in those days by many as a heterosexual thing and didn't fit into the gay sexual revolution), that I didn't think anything of it. Even when I became aware that I had no control over my actions, I had no behavioral framework to place it in, and so just felt helpless. It was only years later when I first heard the words "sexual compulsive" from a friend who had just started attending a 12-step program for sex addicts that the light bulb went on in my head and I said, "So that's why I haven't been able to stop this degrading behavior." From that day onward for many years I attended 12-step meetings and my life was given back to me.

Even today, with all the publicity about sex addiction, there are many men and even some women who are sex addicts but are in denial. Men, especially gay man, think the concept of sex addiction bizarre. They think men being randy and promiscuous is the natural order of things ... and at some level they are right. But we are not animals; we are humans and we do what we do not because of the natural urges that drive animals but for psychological reasons that are distinctly human.

Regardless what the reasons are for wanting to have sex outside your relationship, if you cannot stop that activity and if you truly love your spouse/significant other, then you must confide in your partner and decide together how your lives will move forward. If you do not truly love your partner, then you must break off the relationship for even if your partner would consent to this situation, it will cause suffering both for your partner and yourself. A relationship is built on trust. Once that trust is broken, it is not fair to continue and cause harm.

FAMILY RELATIONSHIPS

A recent *New Yorker* cartoon shows a mother sitting on her young son's bed with her arm around him saying, "Heavens no, sweetie – my love for you has tons of conditions."[24] The cartoon succinctly reflects an unfortunate reality ... the main element that is missing in so many family relationships, be it between siblings or parent and child, is unconditional love and compassion. There is a reason why there are countless novels, plays, and movies about family conflict ... it's a cultural reality.

There will always be sibling rivalry and a certain amount of tension between parents and children, as well as between spouses ... that's just a function of our biological and evolutionary makeup. But such tension can exist within an atmosphere of unconditional love and compassion ... the two are not mutually exclusive.

There are three situations that I will address in this section. The first is how, if your relationship with siblings or parents has been fraught with anger and pain because of your childhood experiences, do you endow those relationships now with unconditional love and compassion. The second is how, if problems in your relationship with your adult children or siblings are a result of pain you brought about in the past, you can change this dynamic. The last is how you, as a parent or spouse, can foster the growth of such an atmosphere in your home.

Improving your relationship with parents and siblings can come about in various ways. The first thing to remember is that your parents and siblings are all human beings. Often we do things with the best of intentions, but they turn out poorly and do harm. It is the rare parent that intentionally inflicts harm, psychological or otherwise, on his or her children. Also, being human, we often blurt out,

---

[24] E. F. Lake, *The New Yorker*, June 6, 2011, p.55

especially in moments of anger or frustration, words that we really don't mean; children especially have the capacity for being very nasty and hurtful. And as the sign in my father's office used to say, "A word once spoken is like a stone thrown ... it cannot be recalled." The impact stays with us often for a lifetime.

Think carefully about what really happened way back when that caused you to carry around so much pain. Chances are you will realize that your reaction to the events was caused by your inability as a child to correctly characterize the events and that when you now see them clearly for what they were, you will find it in your heart to forgive.

Let me briefly describe an example from my own life. For a variety of reasons I came to feel unloved by my father as a child. This pain and the insecurity that flowed from it stayed with me for most of my adult life and caused me much suffering and social dysfunction. It was only much later in life that I understood that I, as a child, had misinterpreted various things as meaning that he didn't love me. But that was in fact not the case.

So strong was my emotional separation from my father that even when I received written evidence of his past love for me, it didn't even register. It was only after having come to understand the true facts that, after coming upon these letters again while cleaning out my files one day, I realized the enormity of my error and the huge loss I had suffered as a result.

Next, cultivate a compassionate heart towards the siblings or parent(s) that you have felt anger towards. Remember the teaching, as discussed earlier, that we are all products of our environment, of our learned experience, and that we don't have the control over our lives that we think we have.

Your parents are or were the products of their own upbringing and other learned experiences. The fact that what they did caused you pain does not negate their love for you. Likewise, each child in a family is different. Yes, you were all raised in the same family, but the learned experiences that each child receives are still often quite different ... whether because your parents' life changed in some way or just because of the position of each child in the family. When you remember this teaching, you will be able to have compassion towards your siblings and parents, just as you hopefully have learned to have compassion for yourself and others.

But what if you as parent has been the one who has caused pain to your now-adult child or children, or in the past caused your parents or siblings pain? The first step in the process is to look back over your relationship with your family with great clarity in light of what you have read in this book. This can be difficult, both in a practical sense and emotionally. But remember that the point is not to find fault with yourself but to understand, for example, that even a very well-meaning parent can do things which unintentionally harm their child. It is not your fault in a moral sense; it is a result of the way in which you were raised and the culture in which we live. But the parent is nevertheless almost always the immediate causal agent.

Once you have figured out what you did ... it could be one thing, it could be many; it could have happened over a very short time frame or it could have been going on for years ... the next step in the process is to make amends.

Making amends ... heartfully acknowledging that there are things you did which caused pain ... will in most circumstances open the door to healthy communication and result in healing. There are three things that are critical when making amends: your acknowledgment must be unequivocal; state that however it may have appeared at the time you always loved the person and had his or her best interest at heart; and you must sincerely and abjectly apologize for the pain that you have caused over the years.

The best format to use when making amends is to start with a letter. By saying it in a letter rather than talking to the person, you will have the chance to review your words and make sure that you are communicating what you mean to communicate. It will also give the person a chance to digest what you have said.

Start the letter with something to the effect of, "I am writing to apologize for the pain I have caused you." Being upfront about the nature of the letter is critical to insuring that even if your relationship is very bad, possibly you are totally estranged, the letter will be read. Perhaps initially out of curiosity and disbelief. But if you have been very honest, open, and heartfelt in the letter, it will ultimately have the desired effect.

While it will be natural for you to want to explain why you did what you did ... and this can greatly aid healing ... remember that it is critical that your acknowledgment must remain unequivocal. It cannot appear to the person that you are making excuses. Thus when you try to explain yourself it should be in the context of, "This does not excuse what I did, but it is important for you to know how this came to be." And then explain what ... whether it was something from your own upbringing or stress you were under at the time or whatever ... caused you to act as you did.

Your letter should cause the person to think carefully about what really happened way back when that caused him or her to carry around so much pain. Chances are they will realize that their reaction to the events was caused by their inability at the time to correctly characterize the events and that when they now see them clearly for what they were, they will find it in their heart to forgive.

The final act of healing these wounds can be achieved through the Tibetan practice of "tonglen," giving and receiving ... taking on the suffering and pain of others and giving them your happiness, wellbeing, and peace of mind.

As I discussed earlier, Sogyal Rinpoche recommends starting this practice by first doing it for yourself.[25] Before one can have such loving kindness for others, one has to have it for oneself.

Once you have done the two exercises he suggests, Rinpoche instructs to let your heart open and extend the love that flows from it to your parents, your siblings, your friends, indeed all people and receive their pain. In my example, I did this towards my father and it proved to be the final step in a long healing process that had begun as part of my Buddhist practice.

If you desire to replace the anger and resentment in your heart with love and compassion, it is in your power to do so, without the involvement of anyone else. External circumstances do not need to change, just your view of and reaction to those circumstances, past or present.

The second situation to be addressed here is how you, as a parent and spouse, can foster the growth of an atmosphere of unconditional love and compassion in your home now. The most important way is by example. In your interactions with your spouse/significant other and children, always show compassion and unconditional love.

The Fourth Precept as interpreted by Thich Nhat Hanh says,

> "Aware of the suffering caused by unmindful speech and the inability to listen to others, I am committed to cultivating loving speech and deep listening ..."

What is missing so often within the family, and of course elsewhere, is deep listening and loving speech. Do you listen deeply to your children when they speak, which involves more than just hearing what they say? And do you always speak to them with loving kindness?

---

[25] See pages 23-25 of this book.

When you have a difference of opinion or you feel your children need direction, always do it within a loving context. The point that needs to be clearly felt is that although there are differences or criticisms, they do not disturb your underlying feelings of unconditional love and compassion. This is why a raised voice is never the right way to deliver criticism; it communicates anger and annoyance, not unconditional love and compassion. If you act consistently in this manner, then if you happen to witness your children acting towards each other badly, you can point to your example and explain the coexistence between rivalry or disagreement on the one hand and unconditional love and compassion on the other and the need to watch what one says.

Another way to foster such an atmosphere is to encourage activities in which the family members compliment each other, acting as a community, rather than compete with each other all the time as individuals. Much has been made of the development of team spirit in the workplace. The same approach is much needed within the contemporary home. In the past when all children had their chores to do, this teamwork was taken for granted; now it is typically nonexistent.

Given current trends in our culture, it is important to note that one does not build this atmosphere, or help your children, by not offering criticism. Unconditional love does not mean uncritical love. Much has been written about how the current generation of teenagers and 20-somethings feel that they have everything coming to them and that they can do no wrong. They are accused of being intoxicated by self-esteem and parents are accused of aiding and abetting this state by a lack of parental criticism and control.

But in a cruel irony, while a display of bravado and feelings of being special may be common, this is not due to their increase in self-esteem. On the contrary, it is yet further evidence of how insecure and hollow our children's lives have become.

It is a well-known psychological fact that having a huge ego is typically a façade, a coping mechanism for deep feelings of insecurity and anxiety. And the size of the ego and extent of aggression is directly related to the amount of insecurity.

Many writers have noted that the generation of people now in their 20s grew up bathed in praise and messages that they are special. While it may well be that such action on the part of parents was meant to increase self-esteem, in fact it often increases insecurity. When a child is told he is special, but feels deep down that he is not because the praise is not grounded on anything specific or is just absurdly effusive, he feels he is being told that he is expected to be special and thus feels under pressure to indeed be special, creating huge insecurities. Or the child feels that words are not to be trusted, creating a feeling of cynicism and insecurity.

If we were to search for a poster child for this American feeling of exceptionalism, we would have to look no further than George W. Bush. While I have no idea how he was raised, he certainly would have had the burden of feeling that he was supposed to be special because of his family's history.

Instead, he knew he didn't measure up and failed at one thing after another. But he did find the gift of gab, of giving the impression that he was very sure of himself. As President, he certainly displayed great bravado and certainty ... he was "the Decider" ... but it was such a pathetic façade. One just had to look into his eyes and watch his facial expressions to know that here was a man who felt totally insecure and out of his element.

If children do something that warrants praise or positive notice, they should be given that feedback clearly based on specific behavior or accomplishment. Your children need to feel that you believe in them, and that belief needs to be based on something tangible. But if a child warrants criticism or disciplining, that should also be given clearly based on specific behavior and always within the context of unconditional love and compassion. In that regard, it is helpful if possible to make a positive comment before offering the criticism. Above all, you as a parent or a spouse must be consistent in your interactions.

There is another caveat regarding providing others with helpful advice or criticism ... be sure that your actions are not an expression of your ego. If you are a worry-wort, if you are always worried about your child or spouse doing something that will harm them in some way, if you try to protect them from such problems, the chances are that this is largely an expression of your ego. You want to feel that you are helpful, that you can solve problems, that you can keep the person from harms way. While this sounds like benevolent action, it is your ego working.

The reality is that your child or spouse needs to find out for themselves what works and what doesn't. That will undoubtedly involve some pain, because we don't always make the right decisions or are careless. But the only way to grow is to learn from mistakes, and unfortunately they usually have to be our own. The only way to gain self-confidence is to do things yourself. If your child or spouse feels that you don't have faith in their ability to tackle things themselves, that you micromanage their activity, then they will not gain that all-important self-confidence.

The line that separates helpful advice and criticism from self-confidence-robbing comments is the pattern of activity. Occasional advice or criticism if properly given as suggested above is probably not a manifestation of your ego and can indeed be helpful. However, if you find that you are constantly concerned about your child or spouse and frequently make comments, then that behavior crosses the line.

Even when making occasional comments, though, reflect on whether you are listening deeply and speaking with loving kindness, or whether you are expressing your ego. Would perhaps the kinder approach in a particular situation be to say nothing or something different?

This is an area of family interaction that is full of minefields. Don't expect perfection from yourself; undoubtedly you will make some wrong choices. But try to be as aware as possible of these issues so that for the most part you will act in what is truly the best interest of your child or spouse.

OTHERS

During the course of every day of our lives, we come into contact with people in many different circumstances ... people who are friends or acquaintances, strangers we see on the street, or people that we read about or see in the news. We react to this stream of humanity in a variety of ways that usually boil down to feelings of either like or dislike, or on occasion even fear.

These reactions are typically unthinking, automatic thoughts based on our learned experience. But although they may be unthinking, they are definitely products of our ego mind. And they have a profound impact on our relationship with the world around us, and more importantly on our own feelings of security.

There is a classic Chinese poem that says in part:

> *If you would clearly see the truth, discard opinions pro and con,*
> *To founder in dislike and like is nothing but the mind's disease,*
> *And not to see the Way's deep truth disturbs the mind's essential peace.*[26]

This automatic categorization of people into like and dislike harms us in several related ways. First, it sets up an "us v. them" dynamic, in which we are separated from all those around us whom we dislike or fear. And if we feel separated from many of those around us, if we do not feel part of the whole of humanity, then we create a world in which we are lonely.

We may feel part of a group but typically the group feels antagonistic towards or beset upon by the "others" and we share those feelings. Thus we can have the feeling of belonging and yet feel isolated.

---

[26] Roshi Philip Kapleau, op. cit.

Another way in which applying labels to people in an unthinking manner harms us, is that then we can never know who those people really are because the labels stand as a barrier to our experiencing the reality of those individuals. If we do not know who they really are, then we rob ourselves of the potential positive interaction with another human being. This aggravates our feeling of loneliness.

This habit also creates a world that frustrates us because of all the people we do not like … that is, people are not as we would like them to be. They don't do what we think they should do, which feeling often descends into anger at "those" people.

At one point in my practice, I told myself that there was no inconsistency between having compassion for all people and disliking some of those people. One could love people unconditionally and still dislike them.

But I soon realized what nonsense that thought was. That was merely my ego trying to retain a foothold in my relations with the world around me. There is no room in the practicing Buddhist's mind for like and dislike.

This is not to say that we are not aware of or blind to people's actions or qualities. But in having compassion for all people, loving them unconditionally, we are aware that "there but for fortune go I." We are each of us, for better or worse, the product of our environment and learned experience.

How do we come to this particular habit energy? Part of it is clearly learned experience. As the song from *South Pacific*[27] says, "You've got to be taught before it's too late/before you are six or seven or eight/to hate all the people your relatives hate/you've got to be carefully taught." And indeed by the time we are young children, the

---

[27] Richard Rodgers and Oscar Hammerstein II, *South Pacific*, "You've Got To Be Carefully Taught," Hal Leonard Corporation, 1981

biases of our parents and our culture have been firmly implanted in our minds.

But there is also something biological/evolutionary going on here. People have a tendency to want to feel part of a group ... a group beyond family. This desire has both defensive and offensive underpinnings.

Ånd so it is that even when we look at children this habit of labeling others and creating an "us" and "other" dynamic is common. They create these labels in order to make themselves feel part of a group that is superior (in their minds) to the others. Whether it's a group of "mean girls" or "goth geeks," whether they're at the top or bottom of the social pecking order, these groups form a basis for both offensive and defensive protection.

From what one reads in the news, we are experiencing an epidemic of male and female school bullies. While children have always resorted to such behavior, the problem seems much worse now, both in its frequency and in its nastiness.

Which also means that many people, myself included, come to this like/dislike, self/other habit because they have been discriminated against or otherwise feel socially rejected by our peers and society. When you think of all the minority groups or others, such as overweight people, who have been placed in that position, that's a large segment of the population.

If you are a parent, it is thus very important to impart to your children not just the compassion and love for siblings and family that was discussed in the previous section, but the broader lesson contained here. Children can absorb such teaching if they have a consistent role model.

Just recently I saw a DVD in which Edward Steichen, the seminal photographer, told the story of how when he was a young boy he called another boy a "kike." When his mother heard this, she explained to Steichen how we are all created equal and are fundamentally the same, one with each other, part of the human family. This was a transformative moment for Steichen who went on to, among other things, create the world-famous exhibition, "The Family of Man."

If you are a victim of such verbal or physical assaults, the lesson is just as important, if more difficult. It is important for your psychological wellbeing not just to forgive but to have compassion towards those who have been unkind and not to label them, "bad." The fear that such labels generate will not protect you but create a further isolating barrier between you and the society in which you live.

When we learn to let go of this habit of labeling all people, have compassion and realize our human commonality, then we experience people directly and we are at peace. Just as when we stop labeling all things and accept the world around us as being the way it is because it's just the way it is, we end our frustration, and we are at peace.

DEATH

Probably one of the most common representations of death in western culture is the grim reaper. He represents our most macabre fears of death ... cold, lonely, agonizing. Fear of death is common in our culture and is one of the main causes of our samsara. Our fear of death harms us because as long as we fear death, we cannot fully live life and take joy in the present. Instead we are forever agonizing about the future and doing what we can to convince ourselves that we will not die ... at least not in the near future. We know that at some point we must die, and yet we are in a state in denial of that basic fact.

Why are we so fearful of death, which is such a natural part of the life cycle? We fear death because of the images of death we have from our learned experience. When we are children, the grim reaper and horror stories strike fear in our hearts. As we grow older, the actual images of death that get imprinted on our brain, whether from the photographs of harrowing death from disease or violence that we see in the media or from our experience with relatives who have died a long and often lonely death, are unsettling if not scary.

Further, we fear death because we fear pain. So many of the images of death that we have stored in our learned experience are embedded with agonizing pain. It is rare for us to experience either in person or in the media a peaceful death, a "good" death.

When my partner of many years died at the end of a long illness, I received a phone call from the hospital ICU telling me that a blood clot had moved into his lungs and that he was gasping for breath ... I needed to rush over. By the time I got there, he was dead. And while I was sorrowful not to have been there at the very end for him, I was grateful that I was spared the experience of watching him gasp for breath, dying what would appear to be a very agonizing claustrophobic death which would have forever been imprinted on my mind. Instead when I got there he looked peaceful and at rest.

We also fear death because of the great unknown of death. What actually happens when we die? Is there really a hell and will we suffer there for eternity? Is it all just over and there's nothing? We do not deal well with uncertainty partly because it scares us and partly because it is something over which we have no control.

As a Buddhist, we learn that all these perceptions are illusory, that our skandhas are empty of intrinsic existence. Every image that we have of death, regardless how real it seems, is not a reflection of what it means to die because the reality of death is unknowable with the power of mind. We cannot know what it feels like to die. I know, for example, that my partner died what was most likely a physically unpleasant death, but I have no idea what it felt like for him. I know he was tired of suffering ... was death a relief to him, did he have a flash of peace at the end? I just have no way of knowing.

The one thing that we do know is that death is a natural and inescapable part of life. The Buddha taught that everything that arises must fall. That is certainly true of birth and death.

If we free ourselves from these images by understanding their illusory nature ... again, yes we saw what we saw, it happened, but what the experience was really like we cannot know ... then we have no thoughts of death, and when we have no thoughts of death we have no fear of death. It just is. We know that it can come at any time ... tonight or in many years. But regardless when or how, we will be ready because we have not lived our life ruled by fear.

As with all our paradigms of life, shifting our relationship with death usually does not come easily or quickly. But as our meditation practice deepens and we observe more things clearly without the intervention of thought, at some point when you meditate on death, you will realize deep in your heart the truth of the Buddha's teaching and be free of death ... not the actuality of it but the fear of it.

WHEN YOU'RE FEELING DOWN

We all have moments ... some of us more frequently and some of greater duration ... when we're feeling down. I'm not talking about clinical depression here, just the more run-of-the-mill feeling down. Regardless what the specific impetus, these feelings generally fall under the rubric of feeling that you don't measure up.

Why do we have such thoughts? We have them because our culture has told us what is expected of us, whether in the workplace, the playing field, in bed, or just about any endeavor. And if we don't measure up, then in the eyes of our culture, our family, and ourselves, we are often deemed a failure.

But are we really a "failure?" The answer of course is, no. These expectations that we have of ourselves are part of our learned experience and the concept of failure is just a label that our culture has taught us to self-apply if we don't meet these expectations.

These perceptions are like all other perceptions, illusory. They have no intrinsic existence, they are totally dependent on the value judgments of our culture or our family. They may feel very real but they are not. The facts of the particular situation are real, but the labels we apply to those facts, the thoughts we have about those facts, are not a reflection of reality. They are just a reflection of our conditioning by our culture.[28]

"Great," you may say, "but this is where I am and this is how I feel." Yes, but if you want to end your suffering ... and feeling down is without question part of our suffering ... then no amount of pep talks or therapy will change how

---

[28] For a more extensive discussion of the illusory nature of our perceptions, see the section, "Behind the Clouds the Sky Is Always Blue," in my book, *The Self in No Self: Buddhist Heresies and Other Lessons of a Buddhist Life*.

you feel. The only answer is to understand and accept that all our perceptions are illusory, that they have no intrinsic existence.

This is another example of our wanting to end our suffering but not wanting to do what we have to do to end that suffering. We have to give up the infallibility of our ego's perceptions. Which is to say that we have to realize that how we view the world through our perceptions and thoughts is not a reflection of reality, just our thoughts.

Understanding this basic truth, internalizing it, takes time and lots of meditation. But if you intellectually understand the point, then until you have, just remember every time you're feeling down that there is no reason for you to be feeling down. You are not a failure. What you are feeling is just a reflection of what our culture has taught you. Saying an affirmation, such as those I included in the earlier section on accepting yourself, is often very helpful at these times.

There are those who say that we do not have to deny our culture in order to be a Buddhist. But to end our suffering, I believe there is no choice. We live in a very destructive culture. It tears people down by bombarding them with images and expectations that they cannot possibly live up to. We can continue to live in our culture, we don't have to separate ourselves from the world around us to experience peace and contentment, but within our minds we have to seek guidance and solace from our true Buddha nature, not our ego.

WHEN REALLY BAD THINGS HAPPEN

There are times when really bad things happen ... things that are totally beyond the pale of everyday disappointments or nastiness ... being subjected to torture, rape, mutilation, or any form of extreme human denigration. These circumstances are thankfully rare, unless one is caught in the crossfire of war or is the object of a genocide. But we know these things do happen, and on a daily basis.

How does one keep ones sanity in such situations? How does one sustain a feeling of humanity and self-worth?

As a Buddhist, the answer lies in three parts. The first is that a Buddhist would never ask, as Job did, "Why me, God?" There is no God in Buddhism, no all-knowing, all-powerful being to whom we pray for deliverance. We understand that things are the way they are because it's just the way it is.

As I've noted previously in this book, I once asked a monk why, if we are all born perfect with the true Buddha nature inside us, we all suffer. His answer, "That's just the way it is. It's like the laws of thermodynamics." The fact that we may have been purposefully singled out as an individual or as a group does not change that basic fact. In this view of the world, we are not victims.

The second answer is compassion. Regardless how horrible the acts are that are done to us, we have compassion for the perpetrator because of the overwhelming samsara that has caused him (or her) to do these monstrous things. We have compassion because of our knowledge that the perpetrator is spiritually in agony and as a product of its learned experience had in fact only a small window of free will in which to act. Thus we forgive the perpetrator; we do not blame.

The third and most central is our belief in our own true Buddha nature. If we have absolute faith in our true Buddha nature and our dignity, then nothing that is done to us, nothing that we experience, can rob us of that dignity. It is the one thing in life that is not impermanent.

There is a children's mantra, "Sticks and stones may break my bones, but words will never hurt me." Children say this in a defensive mode. But it really doesn't help them ... trust me, I know ... because they do not have the awareness and sense of their true Buddha nature to protect themselves from the impact of the barbs that are thrown against them.

But for a Buddhist, this mantra, revised slightly to say, "Sticks and stones may break my bones, but words and actions will not rob me of my dignity and true Buddha nature," has great significance. If we are free of ego, at one with all things, and experience all things directly without the intervention of thought, then no action of another can cause us psychic or spiritual harm.

What is critical here, as throughout the practice of incorporating the Buddha dharma into ones daily life, is having absolute faith in our true Buddha nature. If we lack that faith, then we cannot really take refuge in the Three Jewels because we do not believe this central element of the Buddha's teaching. If we lack that faith we have nothing to surrender our ego to, nothing to counterbalance its force. If we lack that faith, the weight of our learned experience and our cultural environment will make it impossible for us to make progress on the path.

Please do not think I am being glib by dealing with this harrowing type of experience in such a straightforward, seemingly simplistic manner. I do not minimize the assault such experiences make on ones feelings of self-esteem and humanity ... I experienced an instance of rather extreme human denigration as a child. I am just relating the rock that ones belief in ones true Buddha nature can be and the truly literal meaning of "taking refuge" in the Three Jewels against both the lesser and greater assaults that confront us.

Chapter 4
"Work"

Work. Can anything be more stress producing? I was fortunate that because my upbringing was culturally more German than American, and because the times were not as focused on money, when I chose my career and made changes to its path, the choices I made were in keeping with what I would have chosen had I been a Buddhist and followed the suggestions I make in this section. But even though I spent my professional life working for organizations and causes that I believed in, and was professionally fulfilled, the workplace was full of landmines because it is full of people with whom one needs to interact, people who are mostly not spiritual and are driven by competition and other negative learned habits of our culture. Since I came to Buddhism only after I left the workplace, I was often at my wits' end as to how to deal with the issues I faced and as a result often dealt with them badly.

. . . .

CHOOSING YOUR PURPOSE IN LIFE

When people sit down to think about what they want to do with their lives, whether it's for the first time or as a career change, there are many factors ... some knowingly others unknowingly ... that impact that decision. We live in a culture that bombards our senses constantly with messages about what is desirable, what is valued, which most of us have absorbed as if by osmosis. These judgments are part of the learned experience that forms our ego.

These judgments in their most basic form arrive in the form of labels, the words that we apply to certain activity. One's "work" (as opposed to the work one may do around the house or as a volunteer), is defined as "the labor, task, or duty that is ones accustomed means of livelihood." That is, it's how you earn a living. Likewise, "vocation" is defined as, "the work in which a person is regularly employed; occupation." And "employed" is defined as "to provide with a job that pays a salary or wages."[29]

As you see, our cultural bias is towards activity that brings with it an income ... as opposed to, for example, a housewife/homemaker. The task for a Buddhist in approaching this decision is to remove these cultural value judgments from the process to the extent possible and instead look solely at what is the Right effort[30] for you, whether that be a livelihood or not. That is why I put the word "work" in quotation marks in the chapter heading, and why I used the phrase "what they want to do with their lives" rather than "what career to choose" at the beginning of this section.

Noted below are several "ego" factors, which is to say factors that our culture favors in making such decisions, as well as several "Right" factors, which seek to help Buddhists, or anyone, choose a Right effort for your life.

Ego Factor #1: Money – In today's world, the most important factor that many people consider, albeit sometimes unconsciously, in choosing a career or livelihood is the amount of money they will make.[31] It has become the

---

[29] All definitions from Merriam-Webster's Collegiate Dictionary, 10th Edition, 1996

[30] "Right effort" is defined most simply as activity in pursuit of a wholesome state, which is to say a state consistent with the five Precepts.

[31] Neither of the ego factors cited apply to the many lower and middle income people who have no plans to continue their education past high

number one cultural indicator of success and is of vital practical importance to those caught up in our consumer culture.

And the higher up the socio-economic ladder people go, the more desperate the craving gets. There have been numerous articles written on the fact that many of our professions are starving for people ... not just teaching, but even historically more esteemed professions such as engineering ... because so many are lured to careers in finance due to the incredible financial opportunities available in that field. And in New York City, many in the upper middle class have become so obsessed with financial success that they send their toddlers to cram school to try to insure that they get accepted into a good pre-school, which is the first of many steps on the ladder to a financially rewarding career.

The craving for money and all that it can do for one in our culture is obviously not consistent with the Buddhist path. Any craving is the cause of suffering, and it is the release from all craving that is a central goal for a Buddhist.

That much said, money is indispensable to living in our culture. We need it to provide all the necessities of life (which include health care and education) as well as a reasonable modicum of creature comfort. And it makes a difference whether there is one wage-earner in the family or two.

The point here is that if we were able to be free of our culture's value judgments, we could meet those needs with a wide range of incomes, so that the amount of money one eventually earns wouldn't have to be an important factor in choosing a career. The difference between making $50,000 a

---

school, or even attain that status. Their choices, especially in the current economy, are much more a factor of what is available. And if they do have a choice, the money rewards of the job are typically so minimal as to not rise above what's needed for the necessities of life and a reasonable modicum of comfort.

year, say as a teacher, and $500,000, as a middle-level financial manager, is just more things, especially more expensive and prestigious ones. It is not greater security; it is certainly not greater happiness.

So in this analysis, the potential earning factor of a career, above a certain level, should not be a primary consideration for a Buddhist. To the extent that you and your family can, free yourselves from the culture's value judgments and be content with a simpler, less consumer-oriented life. This is not to say that if your right effort/livelihood (see below) brings with it a high income stream that you should reject it; it just shouldn't be the primary factor.

Years ago, this factor was less endemic and less corrupting. For example, when I originally thought about what career I wanted to follow, and in making various career decisions and changes over the years, the amount of money I would earn was never an issue.[32] As a matter of fact, when I made an important decision early in my career to work for public service organizations and nonprofits rather than taking a job with a major law firm, I made that decision knowing full well that I was giving up the opportunity to make lots of money; having a less stressful work atmosphere and feeling that I was helping people in need was more important to me. But even at that time, while I was not alone in acting on such thoughts, I was clearly not in the mainstream.

The world and our culture are quite different now and the importance of money has grown exponentially.

Ego Factor #2: Status of Career – Status of a career choice has always been an issue, both for parents and for the individual or spouse. The many jokes about parents talking about "my son the lawyer" or "my son the doctor"

---

[32] In all honesty I should disclose that I was single at the time with no family obligations.

were an accurate reflection of the importance that the status of a career had in the decision-making process. And yes, while part of that status involved the amount of money someone would make, it was much more a factor of respect.

For some younger readers, it may be hard to imagine that there was a time when a number of professions were in general highly regarded and imbued one with respect. But that was true, and not just for the iconic doctor and lawyer. It was true for engineers, teachers, and many other areas of endeavor.

But this factor is also not a factor that is appropriate for a Buddhist when making a career choice because it has to do again with value judgments that society places on something. It connects with that part of our ego that wants to be noticed, looked up to, valued. It stems from a lack of equanimity, of feeling like we have no value if we are not valued by others.

This is especially important to realize for women or men who are part of a couple where the partner is working and the question is whether you produce income as well or contribute productively in another way. Our culture has always placed an expectation on men that they work and provide for the family. The prevailing sexist attitude used to be that a woman's place was in the home, cooking and raising children ... which was not considered "work."

Times may have changed in many ways regarding gender roles. But even now, if a man chooses to be the stay-at-home partner, he is looked down upon by many for the same sexist reasons; peers don't think he's as much of a man.

For women, working became more common after WWII, but it wasn't an expectation and usually was done out of economic necessity. The peer expectation, especially for women of higher educational achievement or ability, that they have professional careers is a more recent development that resulted from the feminist movement's denigration of being a housewife and its urging women to "fulfill their potential."

Now there is certainly nothing wrong or against Buddhist principles for a man or woman to work and provide a second income for the family ... and for those in lower income categories there may be no practical choice even if one has the very modest goal of not wanting to live in poverty or maintaining a modest standard of living. The point is that it should not happen because you feel compelled to work by internalized cultural value judgments or peer pressure.

If it's not right for you or the larger interests of the family (see Right Factor #1 below), then you should be free of the compulsion to be gainfully employed in order to have a sense of self-value. One shouldn't have to say this, but every endeavor, including taking care of children, keeping house, caring for the property, tending the gardens, etc., has value when it adds to the wellbeing of others, be it the immediate family or the larger society.

In contrast to the two ego factors that I've just discussed, the following three, what I call, "Right Factors," are consistent with the Buddha dharma and your life as a Buddhist.

Right Factor #1: What Is Right for You – Each of us is different in terms of the things that interest us, the natural talents we have, the things that bring us satisfaction in their accomplishment. Since for most of us the time and effort we spend "working" exceeds anything else we do, it is important to our happiness that we choose an effort ... be it a career, or line of work, or unpaid effort ... that taps into our positive energy.

For example, when I first thought about my career, which was when I was in high school, I decided that I wanted to go into theoretical math because math was my favorite subject in school and I was good at it. I liked the way it challenged my brain and the logical thought it fostered. That was my only thought. How much money I would make, what status I would have were not even blips on my mental screen.

After two years in college, though continuing to excel in my studies, I became bored with math for a variety of reasons. My mentor said it would get better, but I didn't want to take the chance on what would happen if it didn't. So I changed majors to something else that I found interesting and challenging. I was planning to continue with graduate school in this field when my brother, who was a lawyer, asked me why not address these issues from a legal perspective? And I thought, why not, and I proceeded to go to law school. This last choice was probably not the choice I should have made had I been thinking more clearly and carefully, but it had nothing to do with money or status; I just went with my brother's suggestion.

In our culture, so many people regardless of socio-economic status do not enjoy their work and see it as merely a means to an end ... making money. This is a sad state of affairs because such people are being robbed of a source of happiness and self-worth. Do not allow yourself to fall into this trap. Choose your effort carefully with yourself in mind.

This is not a Buddhist oxymoron. The concept of no-self, of the oneness of all things, is about not being separate from the world around you, of applying no value labels or value judgments, of understanding that all sentient beings and inanimate things are in the boat of this world together, of being self-less in ones actions. There is nothing inherently irreconcilable between this perspective on the teaching of no-self and planning a career or other type of Right effort even though this necessarily involves some concept of self.[33]

---

[33] For a more expansive discussion of this topic, see the section, "The Self in No Self," in my book, *The Self in No Self: Buddhist Heresies and Other Lessons of a Buddhist Life*.

Be on guard though, for this can be a slippery slope. If we think about a real-life planning situation in a way that is not wholesome, either because it is not consistent with the Five Precepts or because the origination of our thought is a lack of equanimity, then we are indeed back in the control of our ego. What is needed is constant awareness so that if you see ego factors entering into your decision-making, you can stop and separate those factors out from the process.

Right Factor #2: What Does Your Career Add to Society's Wellbeing – Almost any career or line of work or unpaid Right Effort adds something to society's wellbeing, at least as long as we approach our work with love and compassion for all. Whether a plumber or a cashier, a doctor or an engineer, a homemaker or a wage earner, each of these tasks can add to others' wellbeing, can make a difference in someone's life.

There are exceptions, however. Working for an organization that harms people or the environment, especially if one is engaged in activities that directly support such activities would be against the Five Precepts. This would not be Right Livelihood.

But what if one is not directly involved? For example, electricity companies provide a needed service and improve our wellbeing. So being an engineer working on improving the transmission of energy would be consistent with the Precepts.

However, what if the company routinely lies about the safety of its nuclear reactors or degrades the environment. Clearly an activity that is deceitful and/or harmful. What is a Buddhist to do?

The answer is clear, although not what you may want to hear. To work for a company that compromises the wellbeing of people in any capacity is to provide support and sustenance to that company. Therefore, this is not a company a Buddhist should work for.

Bottom line regarding this factor, since one can have a positive impact on people's lives in almost any "job", with the exception noted, it is not so much the job description but the attitude of the individual that makes the difference between work that is Right effort/livelihood and work that is not.

Right Factor #3: Balance – One of the major problems men and women face today in their jobs is the increasing pressure to give more ... to work almost 24/7. How this impacts ones family life and relationships or ones own personal fulfillment is of little concern to employers today. And given the economic climate today, most just go along with these increased expectations, to the detriment of their lives.

Work is an important part of anyone's life. It is after all where we spend most of our waking hours at least five days a week. However, to maintain peace and serenity, one's work should not be the focus of one's life.

Even if you have found a job that meets both Right Factors #1 and #2, every job is going to be filled with stressors and unskillful temptations. And even if you approach your job in a self-less way and see it as a way of helping others in ways small or large, it will bring with it frustrations. So we need to stay grounded in those aspects of out life that bring us peace and serenity.

As discussed in the section on "Staying Grounded," that means not letting work consume one, carving out time for those things that bring you peace and serenity, and maintaining the focus of your life on those things. The reader may well be saying, how does one not let ones job consume one given all the pressures in today's economy?

When I was younger and would interview for jobs, I used to tell prospective employers that I was a very hard worker and produced a lot in a given period of time, but that my weekends and evenings were, as a general rule, sacrosanct. I would not be available except in limited situations. If it posed a problem with an employer, that told me that it wouldn't be a work environment I would be happy in and it was better finding that out up front than later.

And when in a job, while many of my colleagues were working serious overtime hours, I kept to my word and never received a complaint from my superiors. I did my work and fulfilled or exceeded expectations.

I realize that in today's economic climate, showing such determination will be viewed by many readers as risky to ones financial security. But even today, that is probably not always the case. Consider carefully whether and how to make such comments to prospective or existing employers.

If your job so consumes you that you do not have quality time for the things that bring joy into your life, then not only will you suffer, but your family will suffer, even if there is greater financial security. As a Buddhist, at some point one must say that what you give up is not worth the price.

MOVING YOUR CAREER FORWARD

As a Buddhist, moving your career forward is about doing the best work you can, being professional and trustworthy, not competing against others, and certainly not sabotaging the efforts of others. One might respond that in today's dog-eat-dog work environment, if one acts as just prescribed one will get nowhere.

That is a valid point and I cannot say that that is not a real risk, certainly in some work environments. However, I do believe that doing superior work, being professional, and being trustworthy will in the final analysis usually be recognized and rewarded. Besides, if you want to live your life, including your work life, as a Buddhist, you really have no choice. And if you find yourself working in an environment (one can't always tell during the interview process) where you aren't rewarded for your good work, then as a Buddhist you will either accept that as being the way it is, or you will move on. What you cannot do is succumb to the prevailing culture and act in a way contrary to the Precepts.

Some people may say that if you take the ego out of the equation, most of the "progress" that man has made in the sciences and elsewhere would not have occurred and we would still be living in the dark ages. And likewise, those inventors or change agents would not have experienced the success and reknown that they have.

I obviously cannot say to what extent the ego has been involved in all the various discoveries and other changes that have occurred over the centuries. However, one can argue that most if not all of the major discoveries that have changed the way we experience the world (they have not changed the world, because that is and always will be the way it is; the laws of nature are unchanging) have occurred because the person making the discovery was free of learned experience. He or she was able to see the world and experience it directly, without the intervention of existing thought and labels.

In that sense, such people were at least in the area of their professional work enlightened, they were aware that the five skandhas are empty of intrinsic existence, they are of dependent origination. Whether you think of Galileo, Guttenberg, Newton, Madame Curie, Edison, Einstein or whoever, all of these people were free of the constraints of learned experience, which enabled them to see things directly, unencumbered by the then-accepted theories or practices.

To what extent their egos drove them to throw off accepted theories and venture out on their own, I cannot say. I can say, however, that if they were Buddhist and had absorbed the teaching of the Heart Sutra, they would also have made their discoveries. These were examples of Right Effort, in the pursuit of which energy and mental exertion are applied.

Being a Buddhist does not inhibit or discourage you in any way from doing the best work that you are capable of. If anything, it frees you to do the best. As stated earlier in this book, however, when you engage yourself in an effort, it is important to stay grounded and catch the ego when it arises.

WORKPLACE RELATIONSHIPS

Our life in the workplace is in many ways like the jungle where survival of the fittest is the law. Even if you have chosen your career or line of work in accordance with the Right factors discussed earlier in this chapter, it is almost inescapable that there will be many people in the workplace who have a very different outlook on success and competition than you do.

There will be subordinates who are out to get you either because they feel wronged by you or want your job. There will be colleagues who want to beat you out for valuable promotions or assignments. And there will be superiors who feel threatened by you if you are good at what you do. Such at least was my experience. Not fun!

What is a Buddhist to do in these situations? The short answer is to not descend to their level by reverting to ego-driven actions and instead remain true to your Buddhist principles. It means always being truthful, professional, and compassionate. It does not mean rolling over and playing dead, or just turning the other cheek. If one does not stand up for oneself, few others will.

In the case of the subordinate, make sure that you are always compassionate and provide constructive criticism. Always provide favorable comment, if possible, before the criticism. And always explain why you're saying what you're saying. Not following these simple rules is the primary reason why subordinates are often unhappy with their boss. If an employee desires growth, provide appropriate opportunities when available.

If you have a subordinate who is going behind your back to undermine you, continue to develop positive relationships with those in positions of power over you and let the subordinate know that you are aware of what he or she is doing. Obviously you should try to work with this person, uncover any problems, and hopefully resolve them.

If this insubordination continues, you will hopefully be justified, under your organization's rules, in either firing the person or seeing that the person is transferred elsewhere in the organization.

In the case of the colleague, just do the best you can in your work and wish him well. If you don't have a mentor in the organization, develop one, as that can be very helpful in a variety of ways.

In the case of the superior, all you can do is try and maintain a good relationship. Be careful not to be distant, as that can be misinterpreted by someone who is insecure. Make sure you are seen as a part of the team. However, regardless of the positive actions you take, there will be situations where the supervisor is so insecure as to make your life in the workplace a living hell. Talk to your mentor and see how he or she can help; perhaps a lateral move is possible. If it gets to the point where you have no hope of the situation improving, then it is time for you to move on. On no account should you ever feel justified to act unprofessionally.

In all cases, continue to act in a positive manner and never resort to negative actions. Always remember to have compassion for the people you're having problems with; they are not bad people, they are just people who are victims of their learned experience ... remember, "There but for good fortune go I."

Having worked for almost three decades in a variety of public and nonprofit workplaces, both as regular staff and middle level management, I know that what I am suggesting here is not easy. But if you want to live your work-life consistent with your Buddhist practice, there is no other way.

Chapter 5
Lifestyle

Lifestyle. Since I was brought up more German than American, my lifestyle was and is more a product of my upbringing than the prevailing culture. Indeed, in many respects it ran counter to American cultural values even before I became a Buddhist. As a result I was very aware growing up and as an adult of the peer pressure of culture, and how it made me feel different, apart from my peers. Whether it was the "odd" lunches that I brought with me to school, or the European hand-me-downs that I wore that buttoned on the wrong side (like American women's clothing), or the fact that while all my peers have been acquiring the latest technology, I just am not a consumer and make do with products that are considered antique by the industry ... I have been very aware of the dissonance between my lifestyle and the prevailing one. And that awareness when I was younger fed into my feeling different, of not quite belonging. Culture is very oppressive. For most people born and growing up in this country, it is a natural part of life; cultural values are seamlessly woven into every activity and thought. Its influence may be subliminal, (yes, you see the message but you don't really see it's power over you), or absorbed as if by osmosis, but its oppressive nature is still present. If anything, it is more insidious because one isn't even aware of its power.

. . . .

MEAT OR NO MEAT

Most of us grew up as meat-eaters. That is the prevailing culture ... our parents, our friends, virtually everyone around us were meat-eaters. The taste of a good steak or roast or stew, the juiciness of a good hamburger, and for me, all the wonderful German cold-cuts ... the idea of doing without these was one of the hardest things to accept when I thought about living life as a Buddhist.

Both the temples I attended ... a Korean Zen and a Vietnamese Zen were strictly vegetarian. So I thought that being a Buddhist meant being vegetarian ... until I had my first meal with some Tibetan monks and saw them eat meat!

This is truly a "to be or not to be" question in Buddhism. And there is no clear answer, as the various branches of Buddhism ... Theravada, Mahayana, and Vajrayana ... have different teachings on the subject. The subject is so esoteric and confused that I will not even attempt to make sense of the conflicting viewpoints.

Since the teachings of the Buddha on this subject are in dispute, with one school saying that the eating of meat is not consistent with the practice, at least certainly for monks, while another says that it is, at least for lay people and under many conditions even for monks, I would say that one has choices here.

If your practice follows a particular lineage that has a definite teaching on this subject, then it would seem that it would be best to follow those teachings. However, if you, like me, do not follow any particular lineage, then I suggest that making a decision is a question of ethics.

The first Precept says, in one form or another, that one should not kill any sentient being. Killing is certainly in most circumstances the polar opposite of acting with loving kindness towards a person or being.

I once asked a monk if one could kill a mosquito and not break the first Precept. His response was that the

LIFESTYLE

Precepts are not mindless of context. If one is acting in self-defense ... such as killing a mosquito ... then one hasn't broken the first Precept.

Clearly the answer to this question cannot be, "But I really enjoy eating meat and fish." Ones pleasure does not support taking the life of another sentient being.

So the first question for me was, is eating meat and fish necessary or helpful to maintaining health? As a person living with a compromised immune system, this question was very important to me.

The unequivocal answer after reviewing various sources is, no. Eating a vegetarian diet that includes eggs and dairy products not only provides all the nutrients needed for good health (with perhaps an occasional fish dish thrown in) but studies uniformly show that vegetarians are more healthy and live longer than non-vegetarians. There is no health-related reason to eat meat and fish. Indeed, quite the opposite is true.

Is there some other way to justify eating meat and fish without breaking the first Precept? Even if you eat solely free-range meat and wild-caught fish, and even if the animals are killed in a humane way, from an ethical standpoint it makes no difference. Killing is still violence; a taking of life. These animals are still being killed to feed you.

Which brings up one last possible way to justify eating meat and fish. Theravada Buddhism teaches that the Buddha allowed monks to eat meat that was received as part of their alms if they did not know or suspect that the meat was killed specifically for them. One could say that when one buys meat and fish in the supermarket, it certainly is not killed specifically for you. Therefore, it could be eaten.

As a meat and fish eater at the time I began writing this book, and having believed prior to doing the research for this section that there were health justifications for doing so, and I must say loving to cook and eat meat and fish, I was torn as to the path to take in the future. But from an ethical standpoint, I could not see my way clear to justifying my continuing to eat meat and fish.

The "out" that I just noted above about it not being killed specifically for me just doesn't seem valid. Yes, we live in a meat-eating society and whether I eat meat or not is not going to save any animals. But one could say the same thing for the entirety of Buddhist practice ... it is out of step with the rest of our culture and yet we follow the precepts because it is the right thing to do. My actions may not change the world, but it will change me and perhaps influence those with whom I am in direct contact.

Which brings up the point of what to do when invited to someone's house? I believe in being a gracious guest; I eat what is prepared by my host, regardless whether I like it or it conforms to my belief-system. Also, when I'm traveling and don't have options for good substitute protein sources, I do eat meat and fish, for health reasons.

And so, with those exceptions and an occasional fish dish as noted above, from the day I am writing this forward, I commit to being a lacto-ovo vegetarian. My life in all respects will be consistent with the first Precept.

DRINKING, READING, WATCHING, LISTENING

The fifth Precept states in its original Pali[34] format that one undertakes to abstain from "fermented drink that causes heedlessness." Thich Nhat Hanh, however, broadens the scope to include all types of consuming or ingesting:

> *"Aware of the problem caused by unmindful consumption, I am committed to cultivating good health, both physical and mental, for myself, my family, and my society by practicing mindful eating, drinking, and consuming. I will ingest only items that preserve peace, well being, and joy in my body, in my consciousness, and in the collective body and consciousness of my family and society."*[35]

To me, the key phrase in the Pali version of the fifth Precept is, "that causes heedlessness," or in Thich Nhat Hanh's version the phrase, "cultivating good health, both physical and mental," and "preserve peace, wellbeing and joy." How does this focus impact how one should approach drinking, reading, watching, and listening?

Perhaps more so than in any other area covered by this book, American cultural values/habits run counter to Buddhist values. Drinking, including to occasional excess, is part of the fabric of our social interactions, certainly for men. When we go to the market or newsstand, we are bombarded with headlines and photos in various "newspapers" and magazines that cater to celebrity gossip and exposes. TV programming and movies are filled with material which is not wholesome. The airwaves and rap music often contains language that inflicts pain on others or is about inflicting such pain. The fifth Precept is about how

---

[34] Pali is the language that the Buddha spoke and in which the collection of his teachings is written.
[35] Thich Nhat Hanh, op. cit., p.96

we maintain a Buddhist perspective in the midst of all this excess and unwholesomeness.

With regards to drinking, while later Chinese and other versions of this precept simply say that one should abstain from alcohol, and while Thich Nhat Hanh also so instructs, I would respectfully disagree. First, there is no question that not only is moderate drinking not bad for ones health, moderate consumption of red wine has been proven scientifically to actually be good for ones health.

Further, while everyone has a different level of alcohol tolerance, for most people drinking a glass or two of wine, beer, or alcohol will not cloud their thinking nor impact their reflexes when driving nor in some other way bring about "heedlessness." Thus for most people moderate drinking would be consistent with the fifth Precept. If, however, you have a low tolerance for alcohol or if you are an alcohol addict, then indeed any amount of drinking is potentially harmful and should be avoided.

As regards reading, there is much material out there that is harmful to good mental health. All material that gossips and feeds on the problems of others should be avoided because they are disrespectful and lacking in any compassion. Such material is not conducive to good mental health, at least from a Buddhist perspective. Further many books and articles promote a fantasy view of life, especially in the areas of love and romance, that is very harmful and has, as discussed earlier, created an expectation that makes it almost impossible to find happiness. Such material should be avoided.

As regards watching, there has been much debate about whether or not watching violence in movies and television, or watching pornography, is harmful. I would differentiate between gratuitous and intrinsic violence. The best example of gratuitous violence is slasher movies. Even if they don't upset you or numb you to violence, they are degrading of humanity and show no respect for life, thus being the complete opposite of the Precepts. Intrinsic physical violence, such as say the final scene in the movie, *High Noon*, or the verbal violence in, *Who's Afraid of Virginia Woolf*, while certainly not consistent with the Precepts do reflect life and emotions as experienced by real people and thus have an instructive value. Being aware of the world around us in an important part of being not just Buddhist but human.

Pornography, however, is always harmful. Yes, I know that Dr. Ruth and other sex therapists say that watching pornography can be an aid to having "good" sex or refreshing ones sex life. And that may in fact be clinically proven. That does not, however, gainsay that pornography is harmful. It certainly degrades the individuals who act in the films or who appear in the magazines, and it degrades those who adopt the language and practices of pornography in their sex life as well as their partners.

Sex in the Buddhist context is about the expression of love. Anything that in any way degrades or causes pain to either participant is contrary to the Precepts. Even if a person "enjoys" receiving pain and gets turned on by it, it is still an act contrary to Buddhism. One does not bring joy to an individual within Buddhism by inflicting them with pain.

As regards listening, the issue is more the harm done to society than to the individual. The violent, misogynistic, language of much rap "music" is a case in point. Whether clinically proven as causing violence or not, this type of language is clearly not respectful of women or other people. It is degrading. As a Buddhist, therefore, any rap music with these characteristics should be avoided. Likewise talk radio programs or people you may know who use language or engage in conversation that is degrading or not respectful of other people should be avoided.

As regards eating, need more be said than all that has appeared in the press regarding our nation's obesity epidemic? Whether a vegetarian or not, as a Buddhist one should ingest only food and drink that supports a healthy body.

Beyond these examples, there are for each person other things that they read, watch, or listen to that upset them, that agitate them. Regardless whether such agitation is warranted, whether there is a better way that one could react to those things, so long as they cause agitation they should be avoided. Staying centered and at peace is hard enough without being needlessly agitated by things we consume, even if they have social value.

YOU AS CONSUMER

On a scale of 1 to 5, how avid a consumer would you say you are? If you're in the middle to upper part of the scale, read on. If you're really not much of a consumer you can skip this section.

We live in a society that is built not just on capitalism, but on consumerism. Indeed, our mass culture promotes an addiction to consumerism through clever marketing that results in our craving what we don't have, keeping up with the Joneses, wanting to look sexy or attract someone sexy, and on and on. And we always want more. It's never enough. We are always dissatisfied.

As a Buddhist following the path to end suffering, clearly one needs to get off the consumer treadmill, if in fact you are on it. As with all other areas where we seek to change our behavior, the first task is to be aware.

Think about the extent to which you are a poster child for consumerism. Do you have to have every new tech gadget soon after it appears? Is shopping one of your favorite activities? Do you always want something that you don't have, whether it's a fancier stove, better cookware, a snappier car, whatever? Do you enjoy the built-in obsolescence of things so that you have an excuse to buy a new replacement.

If any of this describes you, start today to question yourself when you go to buy something. Stop and ask if you really need what you intend to buy? Is what you have past its useful life in terms of meeting your needs? Do you need the latest apps to function well? If the answer is, no, then stop the buying impulse and start the road to consumer freedom.

Not only will you have more money to save or spend on important things, as well as less debt, you will be happier and find more peace in your life. Psychologically, our addiction to consumerism has led to a nation of individuals who are constantly dissatisfied with their lives ... whether it's how they look, the home they live in, their wardrobe, etc. There is not a single aspect of our lives that escapes this craving. And this dissatisfaction doesn't just affect those on the bottom of the scale; it affects everyone. Even those who have untold riches are caught in the trap of always wanting more. Consumerism is thus a major ingredient in our samsara.

You won't find much evidence of this dissatisfaction in polls because our culture places a premium on having fun, being happy. Since people feel that they're supposed to be having fun and be happy, that that state is valued by our society, people put on that façade ... not knowingly but as an act of self-deception. Similarly, while there are no studies that document what I am about to posit, I believe that the huge increase in the rate of depression in this country stems less from more awareness of the problem as has often been thought, than from this constant dissatisfaction that people feel about themselves. Indeed, it is not uncommon when people are feeling down to get a "fix" by going out and buying something.

Freeing yourself from the craving of consumerism is a wholesome step on the Buddhist path.

LIFESTYLE

YOUR ENVIRONMENTAL IMPACT

I would imagine that virtually anyone who reads this book will feel strongly about the need to protect the environment. They will be against all the things the Bush II administration did and the current crop of Republicans in Congress are doing to weaken environmental protection. That's kind of a "no-brainer."

But when it comes to individual action that impacts the environment, my guess is that most readers do not do all they reasonably could to protect the environment. Let's take three examples: recycling, conservation, and population growth.

Most communities these days have recycling programs set up in such a way that it is pretty easy to participate. All that it requires is the discipline to segregate the different types of waste that we generate. When was the last time that after rinsing out a metal can you dumped it in your regular trash, rather than setting it aside to put in the recycling container? Ditto for a glass container or plastic bottle or a draft letter you printed out.

If you're honest, you will probably admit that while you often put things in the recycling container (which probably is in the cellar or the garage because most kitchens will not accommodate two trash cans), there are many times when you don't. Even though it may be inconvenient at times, remember to recycle everything that can be recycled. Reducing the amount of garbage that goes into landfills is critically important.

Conservation is an area where most of us probably don't do as much as we could. Let's take two examples again: plastic bags and heating/air conditioning.

When you go to the grocery store, do you take reusable cloth bags with you, shunning all use of the ubiquitous plastic bag? If you don't ... if every time you go to the grocery store you end up with 10+ plastic bags, not only are you contributing to land fill mass, but you are contributing to our dependence on foreign oil, as all plastic comes from oil. So that's two strikes against you.

In the winter, what do you keep your thermostat set at? If it's over 68 and you aren't elderly or sick, then you are wasting energy. Many may react to my proposition as being ridiculous, but it's not. It's just that most of us grew up in homes that were overheated. I've known people who would walk around at home in the winter in their T-shirts or tank tops. It's winter … you can always dress warmer if there is a bit of chill in the air, but really, 68 degrees is enough to take out that chill (mine is actually set at 64). You just need to dress appropriately for the season.

In the summer, most homes and certainly all commercial venues are overcooled. Here again, a thermostat setting of 76 or 78 will keep you comfortable. The main thing is for the system to take the humidity out of the air. There is no need to live in an ice box! And if it's not very humid, you don't even need to have the air conditioning on to be comfortable unless it's in the mid 80s or higher. That may sound almost un-American, but it's true. Again it's just a matter of what we've grown use to. For the last three years, I've lived in a house with no air conditioning, just fans.

And while we're talking about air conditioning, let me say a word about cars and air conditioning. When you're driving on the open road (this doesn't apply to stop and go city traffic), having the windows open is like having a fan cooling you off. Yet when I drive down the highway with my windows open on a nice summer day, most of the cars are all closed up with the air conditioning on. Again, a waste of energy.

But when we look at man's impact on the environment, there is one factor that frustrates all other attempts at reducing our imprint on the environment … population growth. Simply put, there are already more people on this planet than it can accommodate without harming the environment. The population increase forecast over the next 50 years would be devastating for the environment and for people. Forget about global warming, basic necessities like food, water, and shelter will become increasingly expensive and financially out of reach for ever larger numbers of people.

"That may well be" you agree, "but what can I do about this problem?" It's like many of the other issues that have been discussed in this book ... if each of us does our little bit within the sphere of influence we impact, then that does make a difference, even if not in the larger scheme of things. What you can do is commit to not having more than 2 children (which would be replacement population growth).

Perhaps even more importantly, you can raise this as an issue with friends and colleagues. This critically important issue is barely mentioned in the media, and then mostly disapprovingly in the context of China's "one child" policy. Occasionally you will see positive articles on family planning efforts in countries like India. But never is the issue of population growth discussed in the context of the United States or the developed world in general.

Of course the Religious Right and the Catholic Church are opposed to family planning both here and in underdeveloped countries. During the Bush II administration and in many states today, they have had a stranglehold on this public policy ... as I write, there are Republican presidential candidates and member of Congress who want to pass a law that would allow states to ban the sale of contraceptives. This is not a matter of being against the "natural" order of things; this is a matter of the survival of the species, as well as, of course, personal privacy and freedom.

It must be noted that in some European countries, population growth is basically static, and that they are concerned about the economic impact of an aging society. This is because our economies have been structured historically based on demographic patterns of growth; little thought if any has been given to how economies can be restructured to be healthy and strong with no population growth.

There is one other way in which we impact the environment that must be raised ... it's the choice we make about where we live. The environment is (and has been) experiencing two major stressors that are directly habitation related ... ever-increasing urban sprawl and the cities of the southwest overtaxing water resources.

Urban sprawl consumes thousands of acres of farmland each year, decreasing both the availability of local produce and the total amount of food available to feed our ever-increasing population. Urban sprawl also greatly increases our dependency on oil because one needs to get in the car to go anywhere, including often commuting long distances in stop and go rush hour traffic.

In the Southwest, you have 30 million people living in arid areas, including the Las Vegas, Phoenix, and LA metropolitan areas, with virtually no local water resources ... dependent on transported water from the Colorado River. But the Colorado River is not limitless, and with the ongoing drought of the last 12 years and the decreasing Rocky Mountain yearly snow mass (on which the river totally depends), it's capacity now is even less. At some point in the not distant future, water shortages will cause dislocations in the agriculture, industry, and lifestyle of the Southwest. This will cause havoc. It's not a question of whether, but how soon.

So if you're thinking of moving either to suburbia or the southwest, you should seriously consider other options. Don't add to the environmental problem. But if you're already living there, you may well not have a realistic choice to make (especially at the particular point in time of this writing because of the weak economic situation ... people are worried about their jobs ... and the bad real estate market). Even disregarding the current economic climate, moving is dislocating for parents and children alike. However, if at some point the possibility of a move does arise, you should try and relocate from suburbia to the city or from the southwest to another area of the country.

CHARITY/VOLUNTEER WORK

It goes without saying that to honor the second Precept we should give to charity and do volunteer work. As Thich Nhat Hanh's version of the Precept states,

> "Aware of the suffering caused by exploitation, social injustice, stealing, and oppression, I am committed to cultivating loving kindness and learning ways to work for wellbeing of people, animals, plant, and minerals. I will practice generosity by sharing time, energy, and material resources with those who are in real need."

Depending on ones financial situation and whether one is working or retired, the ability of someone to give may be limited. The point is to give what one can.

However, for those whose finances are not limited, who have considerable disposable income, you should ask yourself whether you could be giving more. Do you really need yet another pair of outrageously expensive designer shoes? Do you really need a newer, more expensive car? Or would that money be better spent in a gift to a worthy charity? Millions of people in this country are in desperate need of food, clothing, shelter, and all manner of support services. Increase your frame of reference to the world and the number is in the billions. The money spent on those new shoes or car could change the lives of many adults and children.

But there is an important caveat to be made when giving to charity or doing volunteer work ... if it is not done selflessly, then the action is not skillful and not in accord with the Precepts. If giving feeds your ego, then it is not coming from a skillful place. If a motivation behind your giving is to create an image of yourself as being good, whether just in your eyes or in the eyes of others, then your good deed becomes unskillful; indeed it raises a question as to whether you really have an interest in helping others.

The impact of your gift is not lessened, but its impact on your karma changes. You have not done something bad, but the good you have done carries with it a negative impact on you because it solidifies your ego's hold on you, rather than works to free you from your ego.

Be aware of the origination of your actions, your intents. If you find the origination to be unskillful, meditate on this to purify your gift by uncovering your loving kindness for all sentient beings and things and accepting yourself as you are right now.

Chapter 8
Your Buddhist Practice

Practice. As the saying goes, "last but not least." Ideally practicing a religion entails more than going to church, temple, synagogue, or mosque. It means acting throughout the day in accordance with the teachings of the religion. Even for those who are ultra-orthodox, although they may practice their religion throughout the day in a formal way, they still often don't apply the teachings to their interactions with others in their daily life. Nowhere is this more essential than for Buddhism, which is not a religion (although many think of it as one) but a way of life. That is why throughout this book we have been talking about your Buddhist practice in the larger sense ... how you integrate Buddhist philosophy into your everyday life. But you cannot live life as a Buddhist, freeing yourself from the hold of your ego and learned experience, without disciplined formal practice. It is that formal practice that grounds you, gives you the strength to march to a different drummer than your cultural peers.

. . . .

There are four mainstays to a disciplined practice: daily meditation, chants and mantras, attending temple, and reading.

Daily Meditation

If you want to live your life as a Buddhist, as well as make progress on the Buddhist path to end your suffering, you are engaging in an undertaking full of obstacles ... the main one being that the Buddhist way is contrary to almost all your learned experience and is the opposite of what your ego mind will tell you to do. What you are pursuing is a major shift in the paradigms of your life.

Keeping yourself centered on this path will require great fortitude and clarity of mind. And to have such fortitude and clarity of mind in the face of these obstacles requires that you fortify yourself each day with a formal meditation practice. Your spiritual Wheaties, as it were.

I am not going to go into the how-to's of meditation; there are plenty of books and articles regarding that. The essence, however, of all the methods is sitting with proper posture; being quiet and observing our breath; observing our thoughts, not engaging them; and being aware of our surroundings. Just as important is what meditation is not ... it is not stopping, it is not withdrawing; when meditating one never ceases to be part of the flow of life.

Many people find sitting physically difficult. Either they have back problems, or their knees are sensitive, or their legs fall asleep after a while. None of these problems are unusual and there are ways to sit with good posture that accommodate most physical issues. If someone, whether a monk or layperson, tells you that the only way to sit is lotus style ... and there are some who teach that ... I would smile kindly and go find another teacher. There are many styles of sitting that are equally effective.

It's difficult, though not impossible, to learn how to meditate ... both the physical and mental aspects ... by reading instructions in a book. So if there is a temple in your area that offers a course in meditation, I would definitely take advantage of it. If you live in a larger city and there are courses offered by different Buddhist lineages, you might try several different courses as there are various ways of approaching meditation and finding the one that works best for you is worth the effort.

Once you are clear on how to meditate, then you should set a time for yourself to meditate each day, no matter what is going on in your life or where you may be. I meditate in the morning shortly after getting up. I have found that works well because nothing ever interferes with that schedule, and it works equally well whether I'm traveling or at home. Sometimes I also meditate later in the day.

At the end of your meditation, many teachers emphasize the importance of dedicating its merit[36] for the benefit of others. It is part of the lesson that everything we do we should do for the benefit of others, not to feed our ego, with any benefit to ourselves being coincidental. I read a suggested dedication in Sogyal Rinpoche's *The Tibetan Book of Living and Dying* that spoke to me and which I have adapted as follows:

> *I bow out of respect to myself, my fellow man, my fellow creatures, and the universe, and dedicate this practice to the enlightenment of others. May it be as a drop in the ocean of the activity of all other Buddhas who work to liberate and bring enlightenment to all.*

Before saying the dedication, bring your hands together in front of you, palms flat against each other and fingers together pointing upward, in what in Christianity is known as the praying hands and in Korean Zen is the mudra[37] known as "hapchang of a serene heart." Then bow from your waist while reciting the dedication.

How you come out of your meditation is also important, for you want to carry over the mindfulness and peacefulness of your meditation into your daily life to the

---

[36] Merit is the positive force that comes from living your life in accordance with the Five Precepts, which brings you happiness.
[37] "Mudras" are the various hand gestures of the Buddha found in paintings and sculptures. Each has a symbolic meaning.

extent possible. So when you've finished your meditation, don't jump up and begin whatever is on your agenda. First, sit quietly and continue watching your breath for a few moments. Then gently stretch your body to wake it up from its sitting position. When you finally get up, be purposeful in looking at your surroundings and listening mindfully and continue in that observing mode as long as you can. Move slowly, do not rush.

Ideally, your daily meditation should not be limited to the time you spend sitting on your cushion. Instead, you should try to be aware of your breath and observe yourself throughout the day (for more on this, reread the section "Aware Breath = Instant Samadhi"). That awareness or mindfulness helps us learn ... to see the cause of our suffering clearly, to see the discrepancy between our thoughts and reactions and what really is.

This is especially important when you feel frustrated or angry. As suggested earlier, use the awareness of that emotion as a red flag ... your canary in the mine ... that something has carried you away from your true Buddha nature and stop, watch your breath, and observe. This is important because if you do not train yourself to be aware and observe yourself, then there is no doubt that you will go through your day under the control of your ego and learned experience and will not realize you have acted contrary to your Buddhist principles until probably the next time you meditate. This may make for a powerful teaching moment, but it would be better to stop yourself at the moment when you are reacting to something and change your habit energy response.

While meditation is an essential part of the process, it is very important it realize what mediation can do and what it cannot. Many people get frustrated because they've been meditating for some time, as well as doing readings and other supportive things, and yet their suffering has not really lessened. They were looking to meditation to end their suffering, to solve their problems, and it hasn't. But that is not the function of meditation; that is a false expectation.

What meditation does is provide the clarity to see yourself and the world around you free of the effects of your learned experience, free of your ego. It gives you the ability to discern the discrepancy between what your ego is whispering in your ear and what your true Buddha nature is telling you.

It then is up to you to take this clarity and apply it to your daily life, to things both large and small, and thus to gradually free yourself from your suffering and ultimately surrender your ego to your true Buddha nature.

Chants and Mantras

Because making progress on the path is a struggle for most of us, it is helpful to find things that augment meditation, that help you stay focused on the path and not be waylaid by your ego. This is one reason why we go to temple or a dharma group and read Buddhist texts, in addition to the teaching we receive.

Chants and mantras[38] can be very helpful not just in keeping you focused but on reinforcing your efforts to change the paradigms of your life. These can either be things you have picked up somewhere, or things that you have written yourself.

In my own practice, I have found it to be important, as part of the process of walking the path, to make the teachings my own ... so that they express not just what I've been told but what I believe in with all my heart and soul. Putting some teachings in my own words and repeating them daily as part of my meditation practice, together with

---

[38] Mantras are words or phrases that are used as objects of concentration. Most mantras are derived from ancient texts. But I use the term loosely to mean any text used for concentration, to focus the mind. Mantras can be chanted out loud or chanted internally.

other chants or mantras that resonate with me, helped shift my life's paradigms to the Buddhist path.

I start my morning practice with such chants or mantras because they create a mental environment that fosters deeper meditation as well as mindfulness throughout the day. This part of my meditation can take up as much time as my silent sitting meditation, which may be unusual, but I have found it very beneficial over the past 15+ years. I do not repeat the chants again if I meditate later in the day.

A word about how to chant. While some chants, for example the Heart Sutra,[39] certainly deserve study and careful thought as to their teaching, when chanting, conscious awareness of the meaning of the words is unimportant ... the meaning is absorbed on a subconscious level. But to be effective, chanting must be clear, wholehearted and concentrated.[40]

In most traditions, one chants in a monotone at a low pitch that is within your comfort range (no need to go as low as Tibetan monks). However, in both the Korean and Vietnamese Zen traditions, many chants are sung with a clear melody.

What follows are things I chant daily or weekly. If the chant or mantra is not my own, I have noted the source.

1. *Breathing in, I'm aware that all things are impermanent and changeable and that all perceptions are illusory because it's just the way things are. Breathing out, I release all attachments and take joy in each passing moment, free of all frustration.*

Breathing in, I'm aware of all the wonderful things in my life right now at this moment, am grateful, and accept my life as it is right

---

[39] I have not included the text of the Heart Sutra here because of the discussion it merits. For my translation of the Heart Sutra and a discussion of the text, see Chapter 6 of my book, *The Self in No Self: Buddhist Heresies and Other Lessons of a Buddhist Life*.
[40] Roshi Philip Kapleau, op. cit.

now because it's just the way it is. Breathing out, I release all unskillful desires and am happy and content, free of all frustration.

Breathing in, I'm aware of the suffering caused by my ego. Breathing out, I choose to be free and surrender my ego to my true Buddha nature, thus freeing myself from the known, from my attachments, unskillful desires, and fear, thus ending my suffering and enabling me to take joy in each passing moment.

2. *I am happy and content, at peace in the present and know that if I live each day well, the future will take care of itself.*

3. In Praise of Zazen[41]

> *From the very beginning*
> *all beings are Buddha.*
> *Like water and ice,*
> *without water no ice,*
> *outside us no Buddhas.*
>
> *How near the truth*
> *yet how far we week,*
> *like one in water crying "I thirst!"*
> *Like a child of rich birth*
> *wand'ring poor on this earth,*
> *we endlessly circle the six worlds.*
>
> *The cause of our sorrow is ego delusion.*
> *From dark path to dark path*
> *we've wandered in darkness –*
> *how can we be free from birth and death?*
> *The gateway to freedom is zazen samadhi –*
> *beyond exaltation, beyond all our praises,*
> *the pure Mahayana.*

---

[41] ibid

Hearing this truth, heart humble and grateful,
to praise and embrace it,
to practice its wisdom,
brings unending blessings,
brings mountains of merit.

And when we turn inward
and prove our True-nature –
that True-self is no-self,
our own Self is no-self –
we go beyond ego and past clever words.

Then the gate to the oneness
of cause and effect
is thrown open.
Not two and not three,
straight ahead runs the Way.
....
What is there outside us,
what is there we lack?
Nirvana is openly shown to ur eyes.
This earth where we stand
is the pure lotus land,
and this very body the body of Buddha.

4. *Affirming Faith in Mind*[42]

The Great Way is not difficult
for those who do not pick and choose.

When preferences are cast aside
the Way stands clear and undisguised.

But even slight distinctions made

---

[42] ibid, These are the opening verses.

set earth and heaven far apart.

*If you would clearly see the truth,
discard opinions pro and con.*

*To founder in dislike an like
is nothing but the mind's disease.*

*And not to see the Way's deep truth
disturbs the mind's essential peace.*

5. *Appearance of form,
Feelings, perceptions, mental formations,
Consciousness-ego,
All these things are products of thought,
They are not reality.*

*Instead, dwelling in Prajna Wisdom,
Free of ego, at one with all things,
Experiencing things directly, observing
Without the intervention of thought
To my self—nature I return,
My mind is one with the way,
All suffering and doubt cease.*

*For when the mind is one with the way,
The mind rests undisturbed.
And when the mind rests undisturbed,
Nothing in the world offends.*

*And when no thing can give offence,
All obstructions cease to be,
For things are things because of mind, as
Mind is mind because of things.*

Both at source are empty of intrinsic existence.[43]

6. Serenity Prayer, expanded

   Grant me the serenity to understand the things I cannot change, which is the way my life is right now at this moment, and the serenity to just be.

   Grant me the courage to change the things I can, which is how I relate to myself and to others ... the thoughts I think, the words I speak, and the actions I take. Grant me:
   - *the courage to not run from what is, to not seek,*
   - *the courage to love myself unconditionally and have compassion for myself free of fear, guilt, and shame, and*
   - *the courage to jump off the precipice into the land of nirvana thus freeing myself from the known, freeing myself from my ego, being at one with my unborn Buddha mind and dwelling in Prajna Wisdom.*

7. *And acceptance is the answer to all my problems today. When I am disturbed, it is because I find some person, place, thing, or situation – some fact of my life – unacceptable to me, and I can find no serenity until I accept that person, place, thing, or situation as being exactly the way it is at this moment.*[44]

8. *Grant me the strength to free myself from my past and release all attachment and unskillful desires and thus have the serenity to experience peace, happiness, and hope in the present, lifting oppression and frustration from my heart and mind.*

9. *It's just the way it is.*

---

[43] This chant combines elements of the Heart Sutra with language from "Affirming Faith in Mind," above

[44] SCA, *A Program of Recovery*, New York, 1990

10. *I have faith in the teachings of the Buddha and my true Buddha nature.*

   I am aware of all the wonderful things in my life, am grateful, and know that I have what I need, what is important to me, right now.

   I take joy in each moment, in everything I do.

   I love myself unconditionally and have compassion for myself.

   I accept my life as it is right now, and accept that I have no control. Yet know that if I live each day well, the future will take care of itself.

11. *Breathing in I have positive thoughts. Breathing out I release all negativity.*

12. *Breathing in I go deep within and put myself in the hands of my true Buddha nature. Breathing out, like a bird that flies free I am free of my ego.*

Temple

Because we are attempting to change the way we have lived and thought all our lives and because our culture provides us with no support in this endeavor and no role models, it is very important to attend a temple in your area, and if no temple is available sit with a Buddhist meditation group if one is available, on a regular basis.

I suggest a temple as your first choice because most temples have a resident monk or nun, or a trained lay teacher. While there is a huge range in the wisdom and teaching styles and ability of these individuals, I would say that almost any teacher is better than no teacher.

There is also a huge range in the temple experience among the different lineages. For example, if you went to a Tibetan temple, a Korean Zen temple, a Japanese Zen temple, and a Nichirin temple, you would find more differences in their temple ritual than similarities even though they all share the same Buddha dharma.

Even within a particular lineage, you will find differences. For example, when I first went to the Vietnamese Zen temple I attended for 10 years, the two resident nuns included a certain amount of ritual as part of the meditation service and the atmosphere in temple was very quiet and peaceful. When they left, the monk who replaced them placed no value on ritual ... it was all meditation and dharma talk. And the atmosphere was at times almost boisterous and his teaching method was very confrontational. Many members of the sangha did not like the monk's style and they stopped attending. Yet his teaching was the most powerful that I have encountered.

Because there is such a variation in teachers and in the practice of the different lineages, if you have various temples to choose from, I would strongly recommend trying them all to find the one that works best for you. Sometimes it may mean driving or taking public transportation for some distance, but it is worth it to find a good teacher and an atmosphere that resonates with you.

If there is no temple in your geographic area, then hopefully there is at least a Buddhist meditation group that sits regularly. I say Buddhist meditation group, rather than just a meditation group, because if you meditate divorced from the Buddha dharma, you will not be learning to follow the Buddhist path. Often such groups will listen to or watch tapes of well-known Buddhist teachers to stimulate a dharma discussion. This can be a very valuable learning experience.

Aside from the value of obtaining teaching from a temple or dharma group, the other important benefit from attending either is becoming part of a sangha. Again, because our culture does not support our efforts to follow the Buddhist path and provides no role models, meditating with others and experiencing the fellowship of like-minded people provides valuable support to our efforts to live a Buddhist life and end our suffering.

Reading

There is no shortage of books that seek to guide one on various aspects of the path. While they all probably have some value, some certainly contain stronger teaching than others.

I would not, however, attempt to even begin to put together a suggested bibliography because I am not that well read in Buddhist literature. That's mostly because I've been lucky to have had good to very strong teachers along the way. And the boisterous, irreverent monk I referred to previously did not think much of the learning to be gleaned from books.

There are a few books, however, that I have read that I've found to be very powerful in their teachings, and so I shall list those for your consideration:

Sogyal Rinpoche, *The Tibetan Book of Living and Dying*
This was my bible for years. It is beautifully written, accessible, and very relevant for Buddhists who have grown up in Western culture.

Norman Waddell, *The Unborn: The Life and Teachings of Zen Master Bankei*
While at times this seems like a maddeningly simplistic teaching, its basic truth is very powerful.

J. Krishnamurti, *Freedom from the Known*
This is not an easy read, but it is profound and powerful in its teaching.

If you want to read something about the Buddha's life, I would recommend *The Life of the Buddha* by Bhikkhu Nanamoli. While this is often not an easy read, it is somewhat of a "you are there" experience because the text is taken mostly from the Pali canon. Thus when the Buddha speaks it is as close to his actual words as you can find.

When I read this the first time, there were sections that lifted a veil of misinterpretation from aspects of the Buddha dharma. It is a wonderful book.

****

A few closing thoughts. Not only must we be disciplined in our practice if we are to progress on the path, but we must have patience and faith. Changing the paradigms that have been formed over a lifetime and which are inculcated by the prevailing society around us does not happen overnight. And it is made more difficult because our ego is our adversary in this effort, and it is strong. Make no mistake, our ego is not our friend ... it does not want the paradigm to change, it does not want us to be free of it.

But do not read this, or any of my other comments about the ego, and think I am saying that the ego is bad. It is not. It just is, as with all things. It is part of who we are and we should have compassion for our ego, just as we have compassion for our selves. And so following the path is not about getting rid of the ego, or putting it in a cage, it is about surrendering it to our true Buddha nature. My ego will always be part of me, just not active in my daily life.

Which raises an important final point. Buddhism and meditation are not therapy. It is a path to see through the illusions of our mind, to connect to our true selves, and find peace and happiness. If we have serious psychological problems ... for example, if we suffer from depression or addiction ... Buddhism and meditation can play a very central role to ending that suffering, but it is not a replacement for therapy. The stronger our problem, the more necessary it may be to use therapy as an adjunct to our Buddhist practice to help end our suffering.

May the Buddha dharma sustain you as you work to end your suffering and find peace, happiness, and contentment.

I am happy and content,
at peace in the present,
and know that if I live
each day well,
the future will take care of itself.

www.ingramcontent.com/pod-product-compliance
Lightning Source LLC
Chambersburg PA
CBHW051653040426
42446CB00009B/1115